A HISTORY OF
MULTICULTURAL AMERICA

Exploration to the
War of 1812

1492-1814

William Loren Katz

RSVP

**RAINTREE
STECK-VAUGHN**
P U B L I S H E R S
The Steck-Vaughn Company

Austin, Texas

For Laurie

Cover and interior design: Joyce Spicer
Electronic production: Scott Melcer

Library of Congress Cataloging-in-Publication Data

Katz, William Loren.
    Exploration to the War of 1812, 1492-1814 / by William Loren Katz.
        p.   cm. — (A History of multicultural America)
    Includes bibliographical references (p.   ) and index.
    Summary: A multicultural history of the United States, from the discovery of America through the War of 1812, discussing the experiences of various ethnic groups during this period.
    ISBN 0-8114-6275-7   —   ISBN 0-8114-2912-1 (softcover)
    1. Pluralism (Social sciences) — United States — History — Juvenile literature.   2. Minorities — United States — History — Juvenile literature.   3. United States — History — Colonial period, ca. 1600-1775 — Juvenile literature.   4. United States — History — Revolution, 1775-1783 — Social aspects — Juvenile literature.
5. United States — History — 1783-1815 — Juvenile literature.
[1. United States — History — Colonial period, ca. 1600-1752.
12. United States — History — Revolution, 1775-1783.   3. United States — History — 1783-1815.   4. Minorities — History.]   I. Title.
II. Series: Katz, William Loren. History of multicultural America.
E184.A1K297 1993
973—dc20   92-17363
                                                                           CIP
                                                                           AC

Printed and bound in the United States of America

3 4 5 6 7 8 9 0 LB 98 97 96 95 94 93

Acknowledgments

All prints from the collection of the author, William L. Katz with the following exceptions: pp. 78, 79 The Bettmann Archive; pp. 15, 53, 81, 86 North Wind Picture; p. 43 Museum of the City of Mobile.

Cover photographs: (inset) William Katz Collection; (map) North Wind Picture Archive

TABLE OF CONTENTS

INTRODUCTION

The history of the United States is the story of people of many backgrounds. A few became wealthy through their knowledge of science, industry, or banking. But it was ordinary people who most shaped the progress of this country and created our national heritage.

The American experience, however, has often been recounted in history books as the saga of powerful men—presidents and senators, merchants and industrialists. Schoolchildren were taught that the wisdom and patriotism of an elite created democracy and prosperity.

A truthful history of the United States has to do more than celebrate the contributions of the few. Ordinary Americans fought the revolution that set this country free and ordinary workers built the nation's economy. The overwhelming majority of people held no office, made little money, and worked hard all their lives.

Some groups, women and minorities in particular, had to vault legal barriers and public hostility in order to make their contributions to the American dream, only to find that school courses taught little about their achievements. The valiant struggle of minorities and women to win dignity, equality, and justice often was omitted from history's account. Some believe this omission was accidental or careless, others insist it was purposeful.

Native Americans struggled valiantly to survive military and cultural assaults on their lives. But the public was told Native Americans were savages undeserving of any rights to their land or culture. African Americans battled to break the chains of slavery and to scale the walls of racial discrimination. But a century after slavery ended, some textbooks still pictured African Americans as content under slavery and bewildered by freedom. Arrivals from Asia, Mexico, and the West Indies faced legal restrictions and sometimes violence. But the public was told that they were undeserving of a welcome because they took "American jobs" and some were "treacherous aliens."

Whether single, married, or mothers, women were portrayed as dependent on men and accepting of a lowly status. The record of their sturdy labors, enduring strengths, and their arduous struggle to achieve equality rarely found its way into classrooms. The version of American history that reached the public carried many prejudices. It often preferred farmers over urban workers, middle classes over working classes, rich over poor. Women and minorities became invisible, ineffective, or voiceless.

This distorted legacy also failed to mention the campaigns waged by minorities and women to attain human rights. Such efforts did not reflect glory on white male rulers and their unwillingness to extend democracy and opportunity to others.

This kind of history was not a trustworthy tale. It locked out entire races and impeded racial understanding. Not only was it unreliable, but for most students it was dull and boring.

Our history has to be truthful and complete. Our struggle to overcome the barriers of nature and obstacles made by humans is an inspiring story. This series of books seeks to explore the heroic efforts of minorities and women to find their place in the American dream.

William Loren Katz

CHAPTER 1

DISCOVERING AMERICA

Starting with the first inhabitants, America has always been a land of immigrants. When Christopher <u>Columbus</u>, the Italian navigator from Genoa, whose three Spanish ships reached the Bahamas on October 12, 1492, he thought he had reached his goal of India, and he called the natives "Indians." But the Genoese mariner was greeted by people for whom the Americas had been home for centuries. Their ancestors had crossed from Asia to Alaska nine to forty thousand years before and had spread south until they populated most of North and South America.

Archaeological evidence points to the possibility of some African expeditions to the Americas from around 800 B.C. The Portuguese explorer Vasco Núñez de Balboa reported in 1513 finding a race of black-skinned people on the Isthmus of Darien in Panama. Ancient Phoenician inscriptions have been found in southern Pennsylvania and in Massachusetts, indicating the possible presence of traders and sailors from what is now Lebanon in the Middle East.

Sailors from many nations have staked a claim to seeing or touching the New World. In 986 Bjarni Herjulfsson, a Norse navigator whose ship was blown southward while looking for Greenland, may have sighted North America. Fourteen years later, in 1000 Norseman Leif Eriksson found a region that resembled the North American coast. A Hungarian sailor in his crew named Tryker found some grapes, so Scandinavians first called the Americas Vinland. Archaeologists recently have located an ancient Norse settlement, L'Anse aux Meadows, in northern Newfoundland.

Eriksson's brothers, Thorvald and Thornstein, explored the North American coast a half dozen years after Vinland was discovered. Then, between 1010 and 1013 an expedition that included Leif's daughter, Freydis, reached the Americas and may have sailed into Hudson Bay.

*In this old print Columbus is shown at Santo Domingo being welcomed by
Native Americans bearing gifts.*

In 1475, a Danish expedition with a crew that included two Germans and was piloted by a Pole, John Scolvus, may have reached North America. Greece, Ireland, and Yugoslavia have also claimed to have sent sailors to the Americas before the British landed at Jamestown or Plymouth. For example, ships from Dubrovnik, Yugoslavia, may have landed in North Carolina around 1540.

Nevertheless, it was Columbus' landing that completely changed the Americas and the world. His voyages, and the reports about them by Amerigo Vespucci, eventually opened the continent to huge waves of immigration. After Columbus, America would not be the same.

For his first voyage, Columbus recruited men largely from Spain's Basque province. But his crew of 90 included others. There was Juan Arias, a Portuguese, Francis Warnadowicz, a Pole, Blaseus, a Slav from Dubrovnik, and several Spanish Jews—Marco, the surgeon and Maeastre Bernal, a physician. Luis de Torres, the expedition's interpreter of Asian languages, has been called a Jew by one source and a Spanish-Arab by another.

Columbus's expedition sailed from Spain at a time when Spain was at war with its minorities. King Ferdinand and Queen Isabella had just militarily defeated the Moors, Africans who had conquered, lived among, and contributed to Spain's culture for seven centuries. Now these Moors were forced back to unfamiliar homes in northern Africa. The month Columbus sailed Spain also expelled its Jews. For centuries they, too, had played a vital role in Spain's cultural, economic, and political life. The Spanish Inquisition had compelled Jews to convert to Christianity. But by 1492 it was suspected—with good reason—that the forced conversions had simply made many Jews practice their Hebrew religion in secret.

Columbus was a courageous, determined navigator but also a man who accepted the racial thinking of Spain's rulers. The pages of his *Diary* shows he agreed with the expulsion of Spain's Moors and Jews. He also believed in making others submit to the Spanish power. On his first day in the New World his *Diary* noted, "I took some of the Natives by force."

Columbus was surprised by the gentleness of the Native Americans who rushed forward with food and gifts. "When you ask for something they never say no . . . they offer to share with anyone," he wrote. "So tractable, so peaceable are these people," Columbus wrote to King Ferdinand, "that I swear to your Majesties there is not in the world a better nation." To Columbus these qualities of kindness and gentleness were signs of weakness. He told King Ferdinand, "With fifty men we could subjugate them all and make them do what we want." The mariner decided that the Indians should be "made to work . . . and adopt our ways."

Columbus seized and shipped ten Arawak men and women to Spain as slaves. Although slavery had been common all over the world including the Americas it usually involved the enslavement of prisoners after a battle. In time some of these slaves earned their freedom and returned to their homes. But the slavery system that developed in the Americas after the Europeans began their conquests was different. It eventually developed into a huge commercial enterprise that kept people in bondage for life.

On his second voyage, Columbus launched an island to island search for gold and slaves, but by now the explorer found empty villages and fierce armed resistance by Indians. Native Americans had been slow to understand the invasion. Their legends had predicted the arrival of mysterious gods from afar. Were the newcomers with sharp swords and horses these gods?

At first the Indians tried to please the Europeans. By the time they learned their mistake, it was too late. They faced a well-armed foe who aimed to dominate their lives. In 1524, when explorer Giovanni da Verrazano landed on the coast of North America, he found Indians who were "suspicious, hostile, and desirous of obtaining steel implements" to fight the Europeans.

Many Europeans arrived as conquerors, or *conquistadores*, from a continent governed by rich noblemen and kings. Powerful monarchs dominated European nations, and they tried to expand their territories and increase their wealth.

In sixteenth-century Europe most families lived as serfs without land, hope or enough food. Young men from these families were conscripted as soldiers and sent off to conquer the inhabitants of the New World. They were promised land and riches they could not find at home. They joined the conquest with the dazzling thought they might also become rich in the Americas.

Borinquen Becomes Puerto Rico

The Arawaks were about 40,000 strong on November 19, 1493, the day Columbus landed on their island on his second voyage from the Old World. They farmed and fished for food, slept in cotton hammocks, and lived in small wooden houses usually close to water. The Arawaks generously introduced Spaniards to tobacco, corn, and rubber.

The Arawak Indians were peaceful people who had learned to take up arms to defend themselves from raids by the warlike Caribs, another Caribbean society. The Arawaks called their island Borinquen, "land of the brave." Columbus renamed the island St. John the Baptist.

In 1508 Juan Ponce de Leon and 50 Spanish soldiers invaded Borinquen and began to dominate the Natives. After he landed where the present port of San Juan is, he named the island Puerto Rico, Spanish for "rich port."

Spanish officials tried to enslave the Arawaks. When Native leaders urged the villagers to fight, some fought, and others fled to the mountains or nearby islands. Those captured by Spaniards were forced to work, and many died laboring hard for the invader. By 1515 only one tenth of the original 40,000 were still alive. Arawak revolts finally ended their enslavement by the Spanish. In 1513 Spain introduced the first African slaves to take up the workload. People of three races began to meet and to marry.

In 1521 Spain began to turn Puerto Rico into a Catholic colony with Spanish being the official language. There was a Spanish-initiated gold rush, but that soon ended. The island's leading crop eventually became sugarcane.

Africans on the island were worked hard but received some protection from the Catholic church. In Puerto Rico, as in all of Spain's New World possessions, priests treated Africans as human beings with souls. This meant that Africans were as worthy of redemption and admission to church as anyone else. The Catholic church officially sanctified marriages among the three peoples. If a slave escaped to Puerto Rico from elsewhere, he could become free if he swore an oath of loyalty to Spain's king and promised to accept Christian baptism.

Puerto Rico was always considered a rich prize by other European nations. A British fleet attacked it in 1595 and was driven off with heavy casualties. But three years later England sent another expedition that landed east of San Juan and captured the city which they left later. In 1625 Spain drove off Dutch forces after three days of fierce fighting, but only after the invader had burned down the city.

In the 1650s Spain used slaves to build a huge 25-foot wall, 18 feet thick to protect the city. But the citizens of San Juan secretly traded with the French, Dutch, and English merchants from nearby islands. By the 1730s coffee was the leading crop. By 1787 Puerto Rico's population had doubled to 15,000, and there were 30 large towns on the island. Half of the African Puerto Ricans were free by then. In 1796 France and England attacked the island, but the defenders, although outnumbered, drove them off after a month of fighting. ■

CHAPTER 2

NATIVE AMERICANS

In 1492 the original people of the Americas may have numbered between 50 and 100 million. No one is sure. Some ten million may have lived in North America. They were grouped in 600 large and small societies that spoke 500 distinct languages. Some of their political structures were as complex as any in Africa or Europe.

Most Native Americans tried to live at peace with their neighbors, though some nations were warlike and aggressive. Some tortured or enslaved captives. The Aztecs ruled a vast colonial empire and made mass human sacrifices part of their religion.

Conflicts did exist between the Native Americans who shared America's forests, hunting lands, and waters, however, rivalry was confined largely to athletic contests. While the Native Americans did fight wars among themselves, these wars usually did not result in the wholesale destruction of nations or cultures. This was not true in the conflicts between Native Americans and Europeans, conflicts which did destroy whole nations and cultures. The differences between the two cultures was described many years later by Black Hawk, a leader of the Sauk and Fox people who said:

> We can only judge what is proper and right by our
> standard of right and wrong, which differs widely from the
> whites . . . . The whites may do bad all their lives, and then,
> if they are sorry for it when about to die, all is well! But
> with us it is different: we must continue throughout our
> lives to do what we conceive to be good. If we have corn
> and meat, and know of a family that have none, we divide
> with them. If we have more blankets than sufficient, and
> others have not enough, we must give to them that want.

Some Native Americans lived in ancient towns. Others were nomadic people who gathered or hunted food. They feasted on America's rich harvest. Among original Americans few starved or faced desperation, and mental illness was virtually unknown.

An ancient Mexican marriage ceremony as drawn by a European artist.

The Aztecs of Mexico created great cities and a universal educational system for their young. Aztec arts and culture flourished. Their scientists developed a calendar, and scholars recorded the historic milestones of their civilization.

Their capital at Mexico City housed 60,000 people. Aztec engineers drained swamps to build a complicated system of irrigation. The Spanish soldiers were astonished at what they found. One admitted that the Spaniards "even asked whether the things we saw were not a dream."

Aztec armies ruled a far-flung colonial empire of 10 million people. But some subjects had grown resentful. By the time Spanish troops arrived, many in the empire had began to rebel. The conquistadores made use of these divisions to pit one Aztec society against another.

In what is now New Mexico, the Zuni and Hopi peoples built large terraced buildings, each with hundreds of rooms. To guard against attack, these villages were chiseled into cliffs and mountains. The Indians of the southwest developed irrigation canals and dams, worked in ceramics, wove baskets, and made cloth from cotton.

The Indians between the Great Lakes and the Adirondacks

formed the League of the Iroquois. Some 16,000 Mohawks, Oneidas, Onondagas, Cayugas, and Senecas were bound together by a common language. As was traditional among Native Americans, each nation's land belonged to all. Everyone worked, and crops were shared.

Iroquois society had no laws, sheriffs, courts, or jails. Yet rules were observed, and behavior was regulated. Each individual understood right from wrong and what was expected. If a member violated a rule, that member was reminded by the community. If necessary, a person was punished by removal from the village until the offensive behavior was changed.

Like many other Native Americans, the Iroquois did not develop a written language. They could not write promises or treaties, but they honored them. An Iroquois pledge became a sacred trust.

Iroquois women were not only respected, but they selected the men who represented each clan at councils. Then they stood behind them at meetings and replaced any who violated their wishes. Men hunted and fished, and women tended the crops and directed village life. This was in contrast to European culture which held women in mostly inferior positions and denied them any political power.

Children were taught to be independent and not to submit to unreasonable authority. They learned to share possessions and to value equality. They were instructed in Iroquois traditions. Iroquois discipline was not harsh. Children were supposed to learn good behavior through the example set by adults and other children.

Choctaw Indians in a popular athletic contest.

The survival of many European settlements in the New World was often made possible through the skills and generosity of Native Americans. Many early foreign settlements might have perished without the aid of local Indians. This was especially true of the first European settlements along the eastern coast of North America. Indians taught Europeans how to survive in the new environment they encountered. The newcomers were taught how to use fishheads as fertilizer, how to build traps that snared game, and how to construct birchbark canoes. They were shown which animals offered the best food or skins for clothing, and they were warned about dangerous animals and poisons.

Twenty major agricultural products and 40 minor ones were

introduced to the Europeans by Native Americans. Almost half the world's crops today were first grown by Indians and brought to world attention after 1492. In addition to the staples of corn and potatoes, there were tomatoes, pumpkins, pineapples, sweet potatoes, manioc, squash, beans, maple syrup, and a wide variety of fruits and vegetables. Cotton, now grown throughout the world, is derived from a Native American species.

From Native Americans, Europeans learned how to make and use canoes, snowshoes, moccasins, dog sleds, hammocks and how to smoke pipes. The Indians taught them the uses of the rubber ball, central to many of today's athletic contests. Europeans were shown new ways of creating crafts, jewelry, and preserving leather.

Native Americans influenced European ideas about psychology, medicine, diplomatic negotiations, and the environment. European philosophers studied Indian concepts of freedom, self-discipline, and commitment to community. John Collier, a white scholar who lived for years with southwestern Indians, said of their spirit: "Could we make it our own, there would be an eternally inexhaustible earth and a forever lasting peace."

Europeans could have learned more. Indian economic, political, and educational activities were based on community cooperation. Government ruled not by obtuse laws and armed enforcers but by a friendly compact everyone embraced. Along with the corn, cotton, and maple syrup, Native Americans offered the Europeans many opportunities to sample these gifts.

But Native American ideas often differed from European practices. Indians worshiped not a single god but many gods. Religion was an intimate part of daily life rather than preserved as a Sunday ritual. Life was religion, and it had to be savored each day through ritual and reflection. Mountains and hills, lizards and butterflies, goats and flowers represented spirits. Native American families kept their knowledge and traditions locked in their memories. Though their ideas were not written down on paper, the elders made sure they were carefully conveyed to young people.

Nevertheless, despite the evidence, Europeans usually saw Native Americans as having little to offer except their gold, land, and labor. Nor did they make many attempts to understand the Native American way of life.

C H A P T E R   3

THE CLASH AND MELDING OF CULTURES

With the arrival of the Europeans, the Native American nations did more than help the foreigners. They also tried to adjust to the vastly different cultures of the Europeans. This was not easy. European and Native American attitudes about life, land, wealth, and nature were so fundamentally different that conflicts between the two cultures were inevitable.

In Europe 2 percent of all people owned 95 percent of the land. Until 1862 some 85 percent of all Russians were serfs, or little better than slaves, who worked on land owned by a small aristocratic class. There were few if any limits to the absolute power of European kings and nobles. Their only challenge came from a rising merchant class who sought power for themselves. Both the merchant classes and the aristocrats in Europe saw great opportunities for wealth and power in the Americas. Both groups had little regard for the Indians who lived there.

The Europeans who explored, conquered, and eventually settled in the Americas were not all the same. The Spanish, Portuguese, Dutch, English, and French all had different cultures and values, but they did share some common characteristics. Most were out for gain of some type. Most were Christians. And most believed the Native Americans to be inferior beings.

This Native American sketch depicts their battles with the Europeans.

It is not surprising then that early contacts between Europeans and Native Americans were often characterized by violence on both sides. Balboa, crossing Panama to the Pacific in 1513, destroyed villages in his path. When one village surrendered, Balboa's troops used swords to slay the men and then unleashed savage dogs on

600 women and children. In Mexico, Hernan Cortés' army of 500 overwhelmed and defeated the Aztecs. Cortés ordered the destruction of an entire culture. He enslaved men and women, threw priceless Aztec documents into bonfires, and burned officials at the stake. Convinced of the foreigners' invincibility, Aztec monarch Moctezuma called on his people to surrender. Instead, they stoned Moctezuma to death and drove the foreign soldiers from the capital. This rebellion briefly slowed Cortés' advance.

In Peru the four Pizarro brothers found an Inca civilization that traced its origins back to 2100 B.C. This civilization had 18,000 miles of paved roads and thousands of storehouses stocked with freeze-dried food for its 12 million people. A Spaniard wrote the king that the Inca capital, Cuzco, was "so beautiful and has such fine build-

"Protector of the Indians"

Bartolomé de Las Casas, born in 1484, was a teen when in 1498 he sailed from Spain with his father on Columbus' third voyage to the Americas. As a young man, he joined the Dominican brotherhood. In 1510 he became a priest, the first to be ordained in the New World.

When he joined an expedition to Cuba, Las Casas saw native Cuban homes burned and people slain or enslaved. He believed men could not carry out such crimes and still be called Christians. He pleaded with the king to halt a genocide that was devastating Native Americans. The king consequently named him "Protector of the Indians." Las Casas did not mince words in fixing blame for atrocities:

The reason why the Christians
have killed and destroyed such
infinite numbers of souls, is
solely because they have made
gold their ultimate aim, seeking

to load themselves with riches in
the shortest possible time.

He eloquently denounced the crimes of the *conquistadores*:

Tyranny wrought by their
devastations, massacres and
slaughters are so monstrous, that
the blind may see it, the deaf
hear it, and the dumb recount it.

Las Casas faced powerful foes. Officials and landowners stormed at him because he endangered their profits. Bishops charged that he was undermining a holy war against heathenism. But Las Casas never wavered in his crusade for justice for Native Americans. In the New World, he said, it was not the Spaniards but Indians who were the true Christians.

In 1544 Las Casas became a bishop. He had done all he could and felt he had been able to end the conquistadores' worst human rights abuses. ∎

ings it would be remarkable even in Spain."

By A.D. 500, Incas had developed great art, mastered engineering, and irrigated fields that produced seven times as much as modern farming methods. The Pizarros only wanted the riches of the empire.

They pitted Inca subgroups against the central empire and seized Inca king Atahuallpa for ransom. After his people filled a room with gold and silver, the invaders murdered Atahuallpa. Then the four Pizarro brothers fell to fighting among themselves over the division of Inca silver and gold.

The European newcomers also brought valuable gifts to the Americas. They shipped over the first horses and mules as work animals. They introduced new crops—oranges, lemons, pears, apples, sugarcane, wheat, and flax.

The newcomers also introduced Christianity, but they believed that this excused any crimes of the conquest. Missionaries accompanied the conquistadores and brought the "true religion" to the heathens, allowing them, if they were baptized, to enter heaven.

To encourage New World settlements, the king offered Spanish nobles *encomiendas*, or huge land grants, and the right to use the Indians who lived on them. Landlords could work Native Americans as hard as they saw fit but had to agree to let priests convert them.

Some Native Americans had lived free before the conquest and, some had lived under Aztec or Inca control. Now both groups

Bishop Las Casas, "Protector of the Indians."

became captives of a foreign domination. They had to labor under harsh conditions and to pay Spanish taxes. Many bravely resisted the *encomienda* system and the colonial rulers. Yet millions of Indians died during this period from European guns and whips, diseases, and overwork.

Those who first brought Christianity to the New World hoped their religion would help make a better world in the new lands. Roman Catholic priests converted and tried to protect Native Americans. By 1551 Spain had established religious universities in Mexico City, Mexico, and Lima, Peru. Catholic missions began in 1565 in North America with St. Augustine, Florida. In return for their labor, missionaries provided Indians with food, clothing, shelter, and a Christian education. Catholic churches soon stretched from Argentina northward to California.

Many Native American leaders looked upon Christianity as an effort to weaken Native cultural foundations. They said priests excused the conquest and paved the way for European victories. These Native American leaders viewed any acceptance of the enemy's God, rituals, and religion as an effort to undermine Native American civilization and resistance.

Native Americans found many ways to protect their families. Many fled to safety in the woods. Some eagerly took Christianity to their hearts. Others staunchly held to the rituals and beliefs of their ancestors and kept these rituals and beliefs secretly alive at home.

In 1680 the first major Native revolt in North America was an effort by the Pueblo Indians in New Mexico to regain their ancient way of life. After five years of planning, the Pueblos under their leader, Popé, rose up against the Spanish, killing 400 officials and soldiers and driving 2,000 other Spaniards back to Mexico City.

The Pueblos set churches afire, buried religious objects in manure, and killed priests. In acts of religious regeneration, they plunged into rivers and washed away their Christian baptismal names and holy oils with potions supplied by their leaders. Some Pueblo Indians rejected their Catholic marriages and replaced them with ceremonies based on their ancestral rituals. The Pueblos regained their lands and restored a traditional system of cooperative farming.

Popé's rebellion lasted for thirteen years and became one of the most successful challenges to foreign domination in the New World.

But before the next century dawned, Spain again ruled the southwest.

Out of the continuing conflict with Spain, a new group of people emerged in the Americas, one that blended the cultures of Spain and America. Spanish soldiers sent to occupy Native American communities stayed on to marry village women. Africans imported as slaves met and married Indians and Spaniards. Mixed families grew. Children grew up with love for their fathers and mothers. A Catholic church, accepted in time by all, blessed marriages that crossed all the lines of race. A new people, La Raza, had been born. Centuries later, in 1976, La Raza's descendants in Albuquerque, New Mexico, celebrated their cultural legacy with these words:

> Through all the migrations, despite all the pressures to assimilate, we have carried in ourselves the roots and strength of our culture. Our barrios [neighborhoods] in the cities have been rich with the sound of our music and our language, the aromas of our food, the warmth of our customs. In remote mountain villages, especially in northern New Mexico, our people maintained a culture very close to the earth. A culture close to that of the Native American, a culture based on cooperation rather than competition. Whether in city barrio or mountain village, our culture is more than fiestas and tortillas . . . . It is a way of saying: no, we will not be absorbed by anti-human values.

Fleeing Persecution

The Spanish Inquisition reached Mexico in the early sixteenth century. Its purpose was to track down Jews who had fled Spain to the Americas. To escape its agents, Mexico's Jews hid their identities. But between 1528 and 1795, 1,300 people were accused of spreading the Hebrew religion. One man was forced to name 114 Jews. The Inquisition's agents discovered that Jews in Mexico had become masons, shoemakers, tailors, foremen, peddlers, sailors, silversmiths, and goldsmiths.

Many Jews left for Arizona and New Mexico. In 1989 a researcher in New Mexico found women and men practicing Judaism who were still denying they were Jews. After all, such practices had once led to death for their ancestors. ■

CHAPTER 4

PEE DEE RIVER BONDING, 1526

In 1502 Nicolas de Ovando arrived to become governor of Hispaniola, the island that today includes both Haiti and the Dominican Republic. Hispaniola became Spain's first headquarters in the New World. De Ovando's ship also brought the first Africans as slaves to the Americas.

By the next year Governor Ovando complained to King Ferdinand that the Africans were fleeing the plantations and seeking freedom among Native Americans. He claimed these escapees "never would be captured." This spelled trouble to King Ferdinand. He halted the trade in Africans that Europeans saw as vital to providing laborers to till the fields and mine precious metals in America. The desire for profits soon overrode his fears, however, and he allowed the slave trade in captured Africans to resume.

In 1520 Lucas Vazquez de Ayllon, an official on Hispaniola, planned the first European settlement in what was to become the United States. He began slowly and carefully. First, Ayllon sent out Captain Francisco Gordillo to locate a site and build friendships with Natives in what is now North Carolina. Instead, Gordillo joined with Pedro de Quexos, a slave trader, and their men seized 70 Indians as slaves. Angry that the first step at a colony was the kidnapping of those he needed as friends, Ayllon freed them. But he also kept one, Ferdinand Chicorana, as his interpreter.

Again Ayllon sent de Quexos to deal with the people living in what is now North Carolina. The trader returned this time with Native Americans he claimed had volunteered to serve as guides for this expedition. In June 1526, Ayllon sailed with 500 Spanish men and women, 100 African slaves, and some physicians. At the king's request three Dominican missionaries accompanied the expedition to prevent any further enslavement of Native Americans.

Ayllon's expedition quickly slipped toward disaster. One ship was lost and the others reached the wrong coast. Upon landing Chicorana deserted as did the other Native "volunteers." Ayllon's settlement needed outside help, but it stood on land inhabited by people who had been kidnapped by his agents.

Ayllon finally reached a large river in South Carolina, probably the Pee Dee River. There he ordered the Africans to build homes in a marshy area and named his colony San Miguel de Guadalupe. The original inhabitants remained unfriendly or distant. The Europeans at San Miguel de Guadalupe soon became a tragic group. Disease left people too weak to fish. Starvation reigned.

Then an epidemic raged through the colony. Winter winds blew in before housing was in place. Soon angry men began to rally around various leaders, gather weapons, and mutter about mutiny.

Matters came to a head in October when Ayllon died. On cold, windy beaches desperate men shouted and fought. Some claimed the Indians were inciting Africans to set fires.

In November the Africans rebelled and fled to the woods. The Native Americans knew these were not the people who had seized their relatives. They took them in as sisters and brothers.

This old French print,"America," shows Africans and Indians dancing together, symbolizing their friendship and unity.

The 150 surviving Europeans were not willing to face the winter without their slaves or shelters. They sailed back to Hispaniola. But a new colony of Africans and Native Americans lived on. The Europeans had failed to establish a lasting settlement on the banks of the Pee Dee River but a non-European community had succeeded. In their opposition to their European oppressors, the Pee Dee River survivors had found something in common.

Exactly 250 years before the Declaration of Independence, Africans and Indians had united to win liberty. Their colony of San Miguel de Guadalupe was the first permanent foreign settlement on what was to become U.S. soil. It was born 80 years before Jamestown and almost a century before Plymouth.

Other enslaved Africans in the Americas also fled to Indian nations. So this biracial community soon had other imitators. Hidden in distant, hard-to-reach locations, people of color avoided the Europeans who came as conquerors and slave owners. In the wilderness men and women created safe havens for their families.

Florida's Early Explorers

In 1513 Ponce de Leon landed near St. Augustine, Florida, and claimed the area for Spain. When he returned in 1521 with colonists, Native Floridians chased them away, but he insisted Florida belonged to Spain. His mapmakers colored it as Spanish territory, but this was for the amusement of other Europeans.

In 1565 the Spaniards' African laborers built St. Augustine, North America's first city. But Spain established little control over the original Native peoples who ignored their claim of ownership or the pirates who made it their home.

The pathfinders in Florida's interior were Africans who fled the Carolinas seeking a refuge from slavery. Then Seminoles arrived fleeing domination by the Indians in Georgia. The Africans helped them survive by teaching them rice cultivation methods they had learned in Senegambia and Sierra Leone. The two peoples prospered.

An African-Seminole military alliance developed. The British, who had designs on Florida, were annoyed. In 1738 Francisco Menendez, a Mandingo from Africa, and 100 Blacks founded Fort Mosé two miles north of St. Augustine. Menendez's people had been slaves in the Carolinas who won their liberty after three years of soldiering for the Yemassee Indians.

Spain recognized Menendez, who could read and write, as the commander of Fort Mosé. In return he pledged his troops to defend St. Augustine from British invasion forces.

In 1740 Georgia governor James Oglethorpe marched his British troops into Florida. Menendez's militia helped throw back the invaders. But when the British navy destroyed Fort Mosé, he moved his community to St. Augustine. By 1759 he had rebuilt his fort and staffed it with 67 men. Fort Mosé's women and children remained safely in St. Augustine.

While the British imported more slaves to Georgia, many fled to Florida and Menendez. Spain made escape attractive by promising liberty to any who accepted Catholicism and Spanish citizenship.

In 1763 Spain sold Florida to England. Menendez and his people sailed to Cuba where Spain granted them homesteads. British Florida soon had new arrivals. In 1767, 200 Greeks, 110 Italians, and 1,100 Minorcans arrived. They founded New Smyrna and began to grow olives.

Work was hard and demanding. In two years, Carlo Forni, an Italian foreman, led a laborers' revolt against the colony's conditions. New Smyrna lasted for ten years. By then England claimed it, saying Spain had surrendered it by treaty. ■

CHAPTER 5

ARRIVAL OF THE AFRICANS

Europeans who set out for American shores had eager hopes for freedom or sought new economic opportunities. But Africans left their homelands without hope. They had been captured by slave merchants and crossed the Atlantic in chains. For Africans, America did not mean the beginning but the end of opportunity and liberty.

They were packed into narrow ships. To prevent rebelliousness, slave ship captains carefully mixed Africans of different nations and languages. The aim was to make communication difficult and unified action impossible.

To keep captives weak and unable to rebel, they were given small amounts of food and water. To instill fear, any African who offered resistance was met with harsh cruelty or death. With help from women and children, African men revolted an estimated 150 times on the slave ships. "Slavery is a dangerous business at sea as well as ashore," reported Captain Philip Drake. Musket and cannon fire beat back African efforts for liberty at sea. But some mutinies succeeded, and Africans captured ships. Joyful men and women sometimes were able to sail back to their homeland and to be reunited with families and loved ones.

The slave trade was a money-making business. It attracted Europeans and Africans, pirates, kings and nobles. It made people rich and plunged nations into war. In 1493, when Pope Alexander IV divided the New World between Spain and Portugal, he also divided the valuable slave trade between these two European powers.

Enslaved Africans were forced into a slave system that already held Native Americans. But Indians died from European diseases for which they lacked immunity. Now Africans took their places. Some 10,000 Africans inhabited the Americas by 1527. By the end of the century they numbered 90,000.

In 1519 Mexico had a population of 25 million Indians. By the end of the century only a million were still alive. But by 1650 Mexico had 100,000 people who were a mixture of Native Americans and Africans. A biracial people of color was being created.

Enslaved together, Africans and Native Americans tried to break their chains together. On Christmas night in 1522 African and

A European artist captured the horrors of the slave trade that took more than 30 million Africans from their homelands.

Indian slaves on the plantation of Viceroy Diego Columbus, son of the explorer, rose in rebellion. They plunged into the darkness seeking recruits and liberty, but were defeated by armed troops. In the next decade revolts spread to Puerto Rico, Panama, and Cuba.

In 1527 a major insurrection threatened Mexico City when people of color united. Viceroy Antonio de Mendoza reported that Africans "had chosen a King, and had agreed . . . to kill all the Spaniards . . . and that the Indians were also with them." Fifty years later Viceroy Martin Enriquez wrote "the time is coming when these [African] people will have become masters of the Indians, inasmuch as they were born among them and their maidens, and are men who dare to die as well as any Spaniard in the world. I do not know who will be in a position to resist them."

By the 1540s Spain was importing 10,000 Africans to the Americas each year. But often with Native American help, one in ten slaves escaped. "They have more freedom than we have," complained a Spaniard. "We live in constant fear," said another.

Slaveowners desperately tried to pit Native Americans and Africans against one another. "Between the races we cannot dig too deep a gulf," said a French official. Indians were hired to hunt Africans. Africans in turn were bribed to fight Native Americans. To control both peoples, said a Spaniard, "division of the races is an indispensable element."

The Spanish king finally issued orders that Indians and Africans were to be segregated in separate villages. Every effort was to be made to keep the two peoples apart to keep them from uniting against European rule.

An old European print depicts the pursuit and capture of runaway slaves.

Maroon Colonies in the Americas

Throughout the Americas African and Indian slaves fled from European oppression together. People of color formed colonies and alliances in dense woods or mountainous regions. The Europeans called these escaped slaves "Maroons" (runaways) and dispatched troops to recapture them. Military defense against invaders came first. But Maroons tried to live, work, and raise their families in peace. Many sought to return to their African and Indian cultural roots. As farmers and traders they lived harmoniously with neighbors. Some even traded with their former owners.

Before 1700 most Maroon settlements were governed by dynasties modeled on African royalties, with kings and consulting cabinets. Leaders had to protect their villages, negotiate with Europeans, and know when to fight.

In Colonial Brazil two African women commanded Maroon armies. Fillipa Maria Aranha led military forays against the Portuguese that were so successful, the foe decided it was wiser to negotiate with Aranha than try to defeat her troops. She won her people's liberty and sovereignty. In Brazil another African woman led Malali Indians and Africans into battle.

The "Republic of Palmares" Maroon settlement in northeastern Brazil was started around 1600 by

Maroon warriors fought with muskets captured from their European enemies.

escaped Indian and African slaves. It grew to 11,000 people living in three villages. Its long streets, Christian churches, shops, and hundreds of homes were surrounded by three huge walls. Palmares' soldiers defeated many attacks by various groups of Europeans but was finally overrun in 1694 by Portuguese troops. ■

CHAPTER 6

OPENING THE SOUTHWEST

In 1528 the governor of Florida, Pánfilo de Narváez, under orders from King Ferdinand of Spain, launched a search for gold by heading westward from Florida. Narváez recruited 500 Spaniards and brought along some enslaved Africans.

The Spanish force included Andres Dorantes and his large, bearded African slave, Estevanico, or Stephen, Dorantes, age 29. The explorers quickly ran out of food and then patience. In the face of tropical rainstorms, wild animals, and quicksand, brave men panicked. Some prayed for deliverance, and others ran off shouting for help. Many died lost and hungry.

The bad luck continued until only Estevanico, Dorantes, and two other Spaniards were left. The four men spent the next eight years searching for a way to Spanish headquarters at Mexico City. To help the four gain information and food, the African posed as a medicine man with divine powers. He successfully mastered Indian languages and breached cultural barriers.

In their travels, the four met Native Americans who told them about the riches of Cibola, or the Seven Cities of Gold, which was supposedly located northwest of Mexico. The four finally reached Mexico City with their story. The three Spaniards had had enough of wandering and left for home, but Estevanico as a slave did not have that choice.

In 1539 an Italian priest, Father Marcos de Niza, recruited the African to help him locate Cibola. Estevanico served as Niza's expert on the southwest and his advance scout and guide. With some Native Americans and two greyhounds, Estevanico pushed northward from Mexico. He carried a gourd decorated with bells and two feathers as symbols of peace and friendship. Father de Niza instructed him to send back wooden crosses to indicate his progress, the closer to Cibola the larger the cross.

Soon Estevanico's mission had attracted 300 Indian men and

Explorer Estevanico is aided by Native Americans in this mural by Jay Datus.

women. They gave him jewelry and gifts. Without knowing it, the African became the first foreigner to enter Arizona and New Mexico.

The African sent Indian messengers back to Niza with crosses, each one larger than the last. Suddenly, there were no crosses and no word. Then two Indians reached Father Marcos with a tragic tale. Estevanico and his band, they said, were slain by Zunis outside of Cibola. But did the African really die? Or did he, as a man seeking liberty, send some friends back with a cover story and just keep going? The answer is lost in the winds of history.

Nobody ever found the Seven Cities of Gold. But Estevanico lived on for centuries in Zuni legends as a Black Mexican explorer. His travels led to a thorough exploration of the southwest by the Spaniards De Soto, Coronado, and Cabrillo.

Other less known Africans followed in Estevanico's footsteps to the southwest. Many became part of the Native American and Chicano, or Mexican American, heritage. The city of Los Angeles was founded in 1781 by 11 families comprising 44 people, and 26 were of African ancestry. Most of the others were Native Americans or of a parentage that mixed African and Indian, and only two were European.

One founder of Los Angeles, Antonio Miranda, was from the Philippines. Soon Maria Rita Valdez, a granddaughter of one of the Black founders, owned Beverly Hills. Francisco Reyes, another African American founder, owned the San Fernando Valley. He sold it and became the mayor of Los Angeles.

A Spanish census of 1790 found that 18 percent of California's colonists were Africans. They comprised 18 percent of the populations of San Francisco and Monterey, 24 percent of San Jose, and 20 percent of Santa Barbara.

In 1976, for the celebration of the American Bicentennial, Chicanos in New Mexico celebrated their proud legacy with a poem:

> **Birth of the Mestizo**
> The Spanish Conquest
> also brought a new people
> into being —
> children of the Indian woman
> and the Spaniard —
> later, also mixed with
> African slaves brought by Spain.
> Some call us
> "the cosmic people"
> because we mixed
> all the so-called races
> of this planet,
> white, yellow, red, and black,
> to make a new people called Brown.

CHAPTER 7

JAMESTOWN

Jamestown, Virginia, founded in 1607, became the first permanent English colony in the New World. It led a precarious life. In the first seven months famine and disease cut the original 105 settlers down to 32. The generosity of the Native American Powhatan Confederacy of Algonquin nations helped save the remaining settlers.

The Algonquins helped the English adjust to the land and provided them with corn and bread. When the colonists refused to share their metal tools with the Indians, trouble broke out. Jamestown was financed by a London company and run as a business venture. It was populated by settlers who had never worked and governed by Captain John Smith. Men refused to plant, build, or labor. Finally, Smith drew his handgun and ordered them to "work or starve." Work began, and the starving ended.

To ensure Jamestown had products for export, in 1608 its rulers welcomed Polish experts in tar, glass, and pitch. Dutch workers also entered the colony. Captain Smith said his Dutch and Polish workers were the only ones who knew "what a day's work was." The settlement soon attracted French Huguenot, Ukrainian, and Armenian laborers from England.

Some of Jamestown's residents still preferred to steal from the Algonquins rather than work for a living. In 1609 Chief Powhatan confronted Smith over the unending thefts and hostility. He asked him three questions:

Why will you take by force what you may obtain by love?
Why will you destroy us who supply you with food?
What can you get by war?

In 1619 the first representative legislature in the New World was established in Virginia. This legislature was called the House Of Burgesses. It consisted of 22 Burgesses or representatives selected by the property holders of the colony.

Among the colonists who were not represented were the six Poles—Lowicki, Stefanski, Mata, Zarencia, Bogdan, and Sadowski. These Poles felt they should be represented in the House of Burgesses. They marched on the House and the records show that there was "some dispute." Finally, the Burgesses granted the Poles the franchise or vote and declared they were equal citizens of Virginia.

That August another event changed Jamestown. A Dutch ship landed and traded some 20 Africans for food and water. The Africans stepped into Virginia not as slaves but as indentured servants. As indentured men and women they were sent off to labor in the tobacco fields for seven years. After their seven-year indenture ended, these men and women became farmers. There is no record of their voting or being represented in the House of Burgesses.

By 1660 the legal standing of African Americans in Virginia changed. They were no longer indentured servants but were declared chattel, or slaves for life. This meant they and all children born to slave women were forever slaves.

Meanwhile, relations between Jamestown and the Algonquins edged toward violence. In 1622 whites and Indians fought a pitched battle. When the smoke cleared, most white residents were dead, but the Africans were left unharmed. Algonquins had found out that in struggles with the British forces their enemies were the whites, not the Africans.

However, the 1622 attack caused Jamestown's Edward Waterhouse, a leader of the London Company, to proclaim a new

In the European colonies on Chesapeake Bay, white men and women traded while enslaved Africans did much of the hard work.

Indian policy. No longer, he said, would English hands be "tied with gentleness" against "treacherous savages." He called for sudden attacks that burned Indian cornfields and starved their families. After that whites could "enjoy their cultivated places." Within a generation only a handful of Algonquins were left alive.

The British began to use enslaved Africans in other colonies. Slaves not only worked in the fields but provided plantations with all the skills of artisans found in a small city. In Virginia, African labor built Washington's Mount Vernon and Jefferson's Monticello. South Carolina soon had two slaves for every white inhabitant. Georgia had begun with a ban on slavery, but that soon changed. "All unanimously agree," said one British official, "that without Negroes Georgia can never be a colony of any consequence."

British traders brought slavery northward. By 1771 one in seven New York City residents was an African slave. By 1790 one fifth of the city's families owned slaves. In what are now Brooklyn, Queens, and Staten Island, two out of five households had at least one slave.

In New England Africans were required to hold a variety of jobs. In Rhode Island some worked in a creamery factory. Others helped build the famous Touro Synagogue. Governor John Winthrop insisted that slave labor was essential for Massachusetts.

Slaves, no matter where they were placed, became defiant and tried to break their chains. Flight was the most common form of resistance. As early as 1705, colonial New York decreed capital punishment for any slave caught 40 miles north of Albany without a pass. In 1723 Boston slaves were accused of setting a dozen fires in a week.

African slaves and white and Indian indentured servants sometimes fled together. Slave rebellions occurred in both the north and south. In 1740 New York City slaves were accused of poisoning the water supply. The next year four whites were accused of helping them in another New York plot. In South Carolina slaves seized arms, elected a captain, and marched forth "with colors flying and drums beating, like a disciplined company."

Bondage had brought violence and pain to the Americas. Slavery did not produce happy laborers but resistant Americans who thought they should be free.

CHAPTER 8

PLYMOUTH AND OTHER EUROPEAN COLONIES

In the early 1600s different religious groups in England went through a series of conflicts with the official Church of England. Among the groups were the Pilgrims, who, in 1620, left England on the *Mayflower* and settled in Plymouth, Massachusetts. The Wamponoag Indians, led by Chief Massassoit helped the Pilgrims adjust to their new environment. Chief Massassoit was so friendly with the newcomers that he had the names of his sons Wamsutta and Metacomet officially changed to Alexander and Philip.

The foreigners were determined to convert the Indians. They demanded that the Wampanoags follow Puritan laws they could not understand. Massasoit repeatedly silenced those of his people who wanted to protest Pilgrim aggressive behavior.

In 1637 settlers armed with musket and fire launched a night raid on a Pequot village. Many people died while sleeping in flaming huts. To Governor William Bradford the massacre was "a sweet sacrifice" of people he called heathens because they were not Christians.

In 1662 Chief Massasoit died and his son Wamsutta became the leader. British officials seized and questioned the new monarch for hours about his loyalty. By the time he was released, Wamsutta was dying of fever. His brother, Metacomet, 24, then sought revenge. In 1675 he led his Wampanoag warriors in attacks on 52 English towns, and almost a thousand Europeans were slain. The British then marshalled thousands of soldiers. Their spies among Metacomet's Wampanoags murdered his leading chiefs. Other traitors kidnapped his wife and son whom the British sold as slaves in the West Indies. Finally, Metacomet was murdered by a traitor. The Puritans placed Metacomet's severed head high on a pole in Plymouth. It remained there for 25 years as a grisly reminder of the change in relations from the time of Massasoit to that of Metacomet.

This 19th century photograph of Ute Indians shows the racial mixtures among people of color.

Thousands of Indians in North America suffered the fate of Metacomet, his wife, and child. European nations conducted wars against Native Americans in which many Indian men died. Then the surviving widows and children were seized and sold into bondage. Indian slaves were also traded in the West Indies for Africans.

The king of France told his officials in Canada to enslave the Pawnees. He urged bondage for the Natchez along the Mississippi valley and for other Indian nations in the Louisiana territory. In the British colonies, speculators had initiated the Indian slave trade. But its enormous profits soon attracted businessmen, aristocrats, and governors.

Soldiers in Virginia and Massachusetts were given Indian prisoners of war as regular pay or as awards and bonuses. Native slaves were the leading source of colonial revenue in Rhode Island, Maryland, and North and South Carolina. North Carolina's governor Hyde wrote of "the great advantage that may be made of slaves, their being many hundreds of them, women and children."

Since it was not safe to enslave people near their relatives, many were shipped to other colonies. The South Carolina Council and governor listed "Boston, Rhode Island, Pennsylvania, New York, and Virginia" among "places we export Indian slaves."

Throughout the British colonies enslaved and free Africans and Indians began to merge. Among Virginia's Mattaponies, Thomas Jefferson found "more negro than Indian blood in them." Not weighted down by racial prejudice, Native Americans often adopted Africans as equal members of their societies.

In 1721 the governor of Virginia had the Five Civilized Nations—the Cherokee, Creeks, Chickasaws, Choctaws, and Seminoles—promise to return all fugitive slaves held in their villages. In 1726 the governor of New York had the Iroquois Confederacy make the same promise. In 1746 the Hurons promised to return runaway slaves, and the next year the Delawares also promised to do so. None ever returned a slave.

Friendship and marriage among people of color soon led to military alliances. In 1690 British Isaac Morill, African James Dole, and Indian Joseph Moody, were tried together in Newbury, Connecticut. Morill admitted the three men planned a unified Indian and African military assault, assisted by the French, and designed to "cut off" the English.

These alliances continued into the 1700s. In 1727 Africans and Native Americans attacked Virginia frontier settlements. In 1738 Pawtucket, Rhode Island, officials exposed an Indian plot to capture the city and only spare Africans. During the French and Indian wars, a British officer warned of the military danger to the British colonies if the two races united. "Their mixing," he said, "is to be prevented as much as possible."

European officials relied on divide-and-rule tactics. In South Carolina residents were warned not to let Indians talk to Africans or allow Africans to visit Native American villages. The governor announced "it has always been the policy of this government to create an aversion in them [Indians] to Negroes." In 1725, Reverend Richard Ludlam claimed the British "make Indians and Negroes a checque upon each other lest by their Vastly Superior Numbers we should be crushed."

To prevent unity among people of color, the British played and armed one group against the other. For each slave captured in Virginia, whites offered Native Americans 35 deerskins. In the Carolinas the price was three blankets and a musket.

By the time of the American Revolution, the British had halted enslavement of Indians. By keeping one people in chains and not the other, the British hoped the two races would become antagonistic. British officials and traders also introduced to Native Americans the idea of owning Africans. Nevertheless, despite the bribes, rewards and tricks, positive relationships between the two people of color remained firm and lasting.

CHAPTER 9

ALTERNATIVE SOCIETIES IN AMERICA

In Europe, religious persecution and wars were common. Ministers of one religion ruled governments and outlawed other religious creeds. America beckoned as a safe haven for the tormented.

Many Protestant and Catholic immigrants packed up and left for the New World to avoid Old World hatreds. Catholics escaped from Protestant domination. Protestants left from Catholic countries and sometimes fled from other Protestants who did not agree with their beliefs. Persecution of Quakers forced many to leave Europe. Jews left Christian-ruled lands. Ethnic minorities also escaped to avoid being dominated by the majority population that ruled their countries.

Not all 13 English colonies welcomed every type of religious group, but collectively the colonies had within their borders one of the greatest varieties of clerics, and their flocks ever assembled in one place. Among these religious sects were Lutherans, Methodists, Roman Catholics, Jews, Baptists, Presbyterians, Congregationalists, Separatists, Waldensians, Dutch Reformed, Mennonites, French Huguenots, Quakers, Anglicans, and Moravians. Many Africans were Muslims.

Among the Germans, Lutherans were in a majority, but there were also German Reformed, Moravians, Jews, Dunkarks, New Mooners, Schwenfelders, and New-Born. A variety of sects were loosely grouped under the title of Mennonite Brethren.

Many religious groups sprang up throughout the colonies. Some of these groups were tolerant of other groups with different religious beliefs, and some were not. The Quakers in Pennsylvania had a long history of religious tolerance, but the Puritans in Massachusetts had a church-run government with little tolerance for any other religion. Yet liberty struggled to find a light among the

Roger Williams being welcomed by Native Americans.

Puritans. The theocracy's governors tried to silence or cast out outspoken and enlightened followers.

When Roger Williams challenged the Puritan government, he was driven from Massachusetts. A final straw leading to his expulsion was his insistence that Europeans had to buy land from Native Americans rather than accept it from the king. In 1635 Williams, wandering in the snow, was found and rescued by Native Americans. He learned they were proud people, honest and generous in spirit.

Williams purchased land from his hosts to establish Providence, Rhode Island. His settlement welcomed those labeled heretics in other English colonies—Quakers, Jews, Catholics, and a variety of dissidents and non-believers. In Providence there were no slaves, and Indians walked its streets. Out of the American forest, Williams had carved an alternative, diverse, and peaceful community.

Two years later Ann Hutchinson's radical preachings again shook the Puritan colony in Massachusetts. A brave, determined woman, she preached that religion need not be dependent upon Puritan leaders. Infuriated Puritan rulers warned her to cease preaching. Most Europeans viewed public preaching by a woman intolerable and dangerous. She was tried for sedition, excommunicated from the church, and then banished from the colony.

In Rhode Island in 1638 Hutchinson established her own brand of a free society in which various ideas could be discussed. Williams and Hutchinson had extended the shelter of protection to different American religious and ethnic groups.

For runaway slaves, religious toleration was not the issue. They needed a refuge from slave-hunters. The societies of their choice lay hidden from the eyes of European officials. In their alternative communities they had to plan an armed resistance against the slave merchants and slave-hunting posses.

Fugitives from slavery found their first freedom paths led to Native American villages. They often met a hand of friendship and a friendly refuge. Most Indians practiced an adoption system that drew no color line. Along the Atlantic coast some Native Americans took in many slave runaways and made them part of their village life.

Indians and Africans often found they had more in common than an enemy bearing muskets and whips. Among Africans and Native Americans, religious worship was a spiritual force requiring daily ritual and reflection.

For both peoples of color life merged with their environmental surroundings. Neither people had a written language, but both accepted ancient legacies handed down orally by elders. Mountains and lakes, animals, flowers, and people carried life's messages and represented their divinities. Kinship was cherished. Native American villages, like those in Africa, worked as single units of production rather than as competing ones. The economies of both Africans and Native Americans stressed cooperative agriculture, used natural resources to their fullest, and rejected pursuit of wealth. In both cultures economic and judicial decisions, marital customs, and individual roles flowed from kinship and peaceful relationships. Life's choices depended on community needs, duties, and welfare. An overarching "friendly compact," not armed lawmen, kept the peace.

People of color tried to confine competition largely to the athletic field. They saw destiny and community as a single process and tried to avoid or resolve conflict without violence. The youngest were cherished as the society's future, and elders as the source of ancient wisdom. Each person's day was measured by a devotion to community good.

CHAPTER 10

TO COME TO AMERICA

A veritable Tower of Babel walked down the gangplanks of the three-masted ships that landed in the British colonies. Many immigrants left a Europe that restricted a person's right to choose a job, buy land, or earn a decent living. Men and women fled to settlements where they could practice their beliefs. America was their new start.

The New World was awash with new colors, beliefs, and sounds. A rich cultural diversity reached these shores. Although British officials ran the thirteen British colonies, many non-British people lived in them. More than a decade before James Oglethorpe had founded Georgia in 1732, 1,200 Croatian and Slovenian Protestant refugees from Prussia settled there to seek religious liberty. They found it where their creek, Ebeneezer, flowed into the Savannah River.

People other than Swedes lived in New Sweden (now New Jersey), other than Dutch in New Amsterdam (now New York), and other than French in New France (now Quebec, Canada, and the states carved from the Louisiana Territory). The first pioneers France sent to Louisiana in 1719 were 250 Catholic and Protestant German Alsatians who settled in three Mississippi valley villages.

The mixture of races and cultures continued all over the North American continent. Filipino sailors landed in California in 1587. In Spanish-controlled Acapulco, Mexico, Chinese built ships. By 1635 Chinese in Mexico City numbered enough to form their own neighborhood. When the British captured New Amsterdam in 1664, they found that 30 percent of the population was not Dutch. New Amsterdam's first governor, Peter Minuit, was of German and French parentage, and had arrived in 1638 with 23 Swedes and a crew of Dutch and Swedish sailors. The colony's first poet and first bricklayer were both Danes. Half a dozen men, including their underpaid school teacher, were Lithuanians married to Dutch women. New Amsterdam also had its own small Jewish community. In 1633 Augustine Herrman, a Czech, had left New Amsterdam for Maryland where he gave the Bohemia River its name. By 1700 a dozen different languages could be heard on the muddy streets of New York. By then Jonas Bronck had traded his muskets, kettles, some shirts, axes, and six gold coins for 500 acres of Indian land. He honored it with his own name, the Bronx.

There were Belgians in Connecticut, Pennsylvania, and New Jersey. Czechs had homes in Massachusetts, Virginia, Connecticut, Maryland, Long Island, Westchester, and New York. Portuguese had settled in South Carolina, Rhode Island, California, Pennsylvania, Louisiana, and Hawaii (where they developed the ukulele).

Gypsies from England lived in the West Indies and Virginia, those from Portugal in Brazil, from France in Louisiana, from Holland in New Jersey, from Germany in Pennsylvania. Croatians settled in Texas, California, and Mexico. Russians, including Ukrainians, had spread southward from Alaska to California.

The Germans of Pennsylvania

The German settlers of Pennsylvania kept gardens, orchards, and beehives. They probably were the first to cultivate asparagus and cauliflower in the Americas. Since their families were large, they needed all the food they could grow. Everyone, including children, had to pitch in at fall harvest time.

Like other Europeans, large numbers of Germans had sailed to the New World as indentured servants. Once free, they burned with a desire to own their own property.

German immigrants soon earned a reputation for hard work. Their first home was a sod house, the next a log cabin, and their last was an impressive stone structure. Almost as important as their homes were the huge barns they built to protect their livestock and crops.

German Americans carefully preserved their cultural traditions and rich folklore. These became the basis for marriage rituals, interpretations of dreams, and analyses of diseases. German farmers also gained a reputation for great thrift. An English colonial Governor said that German "industry and frugality have been the principal instruments of raising Pennsylvania to its present flourishing condition beyond any of his Majesty's Colonies in North America."

Germans contributed something else of value to a growing America. Between 1734 and 1800 they began the publication of 38 newspapers and periodicals. ∎

Latvians and Estonians lived in Delaware, Pennsylvania, and Massachusetts. Luxembourgers were in New York and Louisiana.

Before William Penn governed Pennsylvania, the Finns who lived there had built the New World's first log cabins, rail fences, and saunas. Poles had come to Virginia, Kentucky, Tennessee, Pennsylvania, Ohio, and New York. In 1679 Albrecht Zaborowsky, either a Pole or Czech, signed as the interpreter for an Indian treaty in colonial New York.

Italians had homes in Georgia, Florida, New York, Virginia, Rhode Island, Connecticut, Maryland, Pennsylvania, and California. Danes, Finns, and Swedes had settled in Delaware, Maryland, New York, Pennsylvania, and New Jersey. Norwegians had made homes in Georgia, Pennsylvania, Delaware, and New York. Swiss settled in Pennsylvania, and North and South Carolina. Slavs lived in New Mexico, California, and Georgia. Jews had settled not only along the east coast but also in Arizona, New Mexico, and Florida, as well. By 1750, Jews in colonial New York, Rhode Island, and South Carolina had built synagogues. Irish Protestants, Quakers, and Catholics could be found in each colony and on every frontier. By 1683 New York had an Irish governor, Thomas Dongan, whose administration was known for sound economic and social policies.

In 1749 Scots made up one sixth of Pennsylvania's population. By 1776 they had built 500 settlements, each with one or more Presbyterian churches. Along with Welsh, Spaniards, Germans, French Canadians, and Africans, Scots were those individuals who roamed from Canada's and Florida's Atlantic shores to the Pacific.

A minority of pioneers were women who had braved the stormy Atlantic to find homes in the New World. In each settlement, they labored as hard and with as much responsibility as men. They handled the muskets, cooked the meals, taught the children and tilled the field. Some became midwives and doctors, printers and poets. Their devotion to family, children, and religion—in homes of every language—helped bond communities together.

New arrivals brought many gifts and talents. Finnish women made brandy from peaches, wine from grapes, and beer from persimmons. Men from Scotland and France became leaders in the fur trade. Swedes brought their system of flour mills, log cabins, organized government, court and jury systems, and Lutheran churches.

Governor Oglethorpe of Georgia (left) is welcomed by settlers from Scotland.

Africans brought their own unique knowledge of tropical agriculture and of valuable herbs that could be turned into medicines or poisons.

In Pennsylvania Germans invented two devices that tamed the wilderness. The Conestoga wagon helped pioneer families scale mountains and ford rivers. Their famous Kentucky rifle—longer, lighter, more accurate that any musket of its day—gave the newcomers commanding power against any enemy. Frontiersmen plunged from the British American colonies into the unknown. In Pennsylvania Polish immigrant Anthony Sadowski became a famous interpreter and Indian trader. His sons, Jacob and James, who changed their name to Sandusky, joined Daniel Boone as hunters and trappers. Jacob helped lay out Louisville, Kentucky, in June 1774, reached Cincinnati, Ohio, in May, and with his brother founded Harrodsburg, Kentucky, in June. He then became the first white man to cut through the wilderness to the Cumberland River and the first to canoe down the Mississippi to New Orleans. A year later two other Sandusky brothers, Emmanuel and John, became pioneer settlers of Nashville, Tennessee.

Italian pathfinder Enrico Tonti had lost his right hand in the Sicilian wars and replaced it with one of iron. He used it to hack his way through the Illinois wilderness. In 1679 he built the *Griffin*, the first large ship to sail the Great Lakes. Second in command to French explorer Robert La Salle, Tonti helped establish the first European settlement in Illinois. Three years later he and La Salle claimed the Louisiana Territory for France. In 1686 Tonti founded the first European colony in Arkansas. Tonti's brother Alfonso led settlers to what became the city of Detroit, Michigan. For 12 years he was its governor. Alfonso's daughter, Theresa, became the first white child born at this distant frontier post.

Explorer Enrico Tonti who founded European settlements in what is now Illinois and Arkansas.

Jean Baptiste du Sable was born to a French father and an African mother in the West Indies. In 1779, after a Paris education, he arrived in Illinois with 23 European art treasures. He used them to decorate the log cabin he built for Catherine, his Indian bride. Chief Pontiac and Daniel Boone were among the Du Sables' guests. Their small fur trading post expanded to become the city of Chicago. When the Indians used to say "the first white man who came to Chicago was black," they meant Du Sable. Robert Harper, a German immigrant founded Harper's Ferry, Virginia. Another, Samuel Waldo started Waldoboro, Maine. Then he sailed back to visit Saxony in Germany and persuaded 40 more families to join his frontier community.

By the time the thirteen colonies became the United States, English inhabitants were outnumbered by others. In 1790 U.S. authorities conducted the first census. They found that of the 3,929,214 people only 60 percent of the whites had English backgrounds. But if the number of Indians and Africans were added to the total, only 49 percent of people in the new nation had English ancestors.

Missionaries, the Second Wave

Carrying little more than their Bibles and a faith in salvation, Catholic and Protestant missionaries formed a pathfinder wave to the New World. Spanish clerics accompanied the conquistadores. Father Junípero Serra began nine missions that became the basis of Spain's California colonies. French Father Pére Marquette and trapper Louis Jolliet explored the Mississippi and Illinois rivers.

To propagate the faith, missionaries often penetrated remote regions before government or military expeditions. They made a better impression on their Native American hosts. In 1645 Lutheran cleric John Campanius of New Sweden arrived to live with the Delawares. He learned their language and became so well trusted that the Delawares called Swedes "Netappi" meaning "our people."

In 1673 Father Ivan Rataj, a Croatian priest, began a decade of life among Native Americans in the Southwest. Half a century later, a priest Spaniards called Father Consag, a Croatian Jesuit, explored the Gulf of California. He proved that Baja California was a peninsula and drew its first dependable map.

In 1763 the Moravian Brethren (who arrived in America in 1735 and by 1741 founded Nazareth, Bethlehem, and Lititz, Pennsylvania) became the first Protestant missionaries among the Indians. The next year Reverend Christian Post, a Polish Moravian, explored New York, Pennsylvania, Connecticut and the Ohio valley. His 1759 *Journal* told of his Christian labors among the Iroquois. In 1793 Stephen Badin of Orléans, France, became the first priest ordained on what is now U.S. soil. In the 1830s he served as missionary with Indians in the Midwest. Reverend Louis Hennepin, a French-speaking Belgian Walloon, became the first European to reach Niagara Falls. He published three books on his pioneer explorations.

John Marrant, an African born in New York in 1755, lived among the Cherokees and learned their language. Methodists trained him as a minister in Nova Scotia, and he served among Creeks, Catawar, and Housa Indian nations. In 1789 he wrote a book telling his life story. By 1835 it had gone into 19 editions. In 1795 Lithuanian Demetrius Gallitzin, the first Catholic priest to take his vows in the United States, founded Loretto, Pennsylvania. In 1816 he became the author of *A Defense of Catholic Principles*, the first polemical work by an American priest. ■

44

CHAPTER 11

SOLVING OLD PROBLEMS

Many settlers in the English colonies left Europe because of the oppressive economic conditions there. Rising above one's class or status was very difficult in many European countries. A craftsman usually followed his father's occupation, and those with no skills were condemned to working for starvation wages and in endless poverty.

To pay for their voyage, more than half of Europeans who came to British America had to sign a contract of indenture. The indentured servant had to pledge his or her labor to an American master for about seven years. In return he or she was promised food, clothing, and shelter. Some owners promised to teach the indentured a skill and provide each with a parcel of land once they were free.

Indentured servants came from all classes of people. Even aristocrats who had lost all their money and social position became indentured servants. The indentured servants arrived in the colonies on crowded ships and often had to undergo a physical examination for contagious diseases before being allowed entry into the colonies. Non-English servants had to take an oath of loyalty to the British king.

Some settlers arrived with no signed contract for their services. Usually, their passage had been paid for by a ship's captain. Once in the colonies these immigrants sold their services as indentured servants to the highest bidders. Prices and length of service were often determined by a person's age, sex, and how much the ship's captain charged for the trip. To find a buyer, some who made the voyage had to promise additional years of service or even offer the services of their children.

Indentured servants could be treated as badly as slaves. They could not marry, visit, or stay out without permission. Masters often tried to take advantage of young indentured women.

Reward notices in colonial newspapers listed and announced rewards for capturing the indentured servants who tried to escape. Sometimes whites servants fled with Indian and black servants or with slaves they had befriended.

After seven years, servants were usually handed their liberty and a new set of clothes. At times, especially in the South, the newly freed servant was given some land. Then a new life began. Irish servant, Matthew Lyon, was once traded for a horse. Later he became a Vermont congressman and one of the richest men in the state.

Life for women in the colonies could be hard, especially for the poor. Wives often had seven to fourteen children, but many of these children died before reaching adulthood. Women on the frontier had an especially hard life, and many did not live to see old age.

Women were one of the stabilizing forces in communities. They, along with the men and the clergy, taught the young the culture of the Old World and the ways of the New World. They helped preserve the language, honored legacies, and saw that traditions were ritualized in holiday celebrations. Women made the thread and did the spinning, weaving, and dyeing, and made most of the clothing.

Frontier women learned to set traps, till the fields, and fire muskets. A few became barbers, storekeepers, schoolteachers, blacksmiths, butchers, and gunsmiths. Some frontier women worked as midwives and doctors, and others became printers.

Some European immigrants found the bigotry they hoped to have left behind had also crossed the Atlantic. In 1654 Jews arrived in the Dutch colony of New Amsterdam from Brazil to a frosty welcome. Governor Peter Stuyvesant refused to admit them into his colony. A heated three-year argument followed. Governor Stuyvesant told Holland's Dutch West India Company that he considered the arrivals "repugnant" and "hateful enemies and blasphemers." But Jewish members of its Board of Directors in the home country insisted he admit the new arrivals. The governor had no choice.

When the British captured the colony and made it New York in 1664, Jewish citizens again had to fight for their rights. By 1730 they had established a synagogue, but they could not vote, run for office, or serve on juries or in the militia. These rights came later.

In Rhode Island, Jewish immigrants had the good fortune to encounter Reverend Roger Williams who welcomed Jews from Spain, Portugal, the West Indies, Poland, and New Amsterdam. By 1763, Jews in Newport had built the beautiful Touro Synagogue.

Perhaps the most despised religious minority in the Americas was the Quakers, or Society of Friends. They infuriated others by their principles. Quakers did not believe that worship services required ministers or rules. At their meetings, anyone could speak. Quakers rejected war or owning slaves as unchristian.

In 1656 they arrived in the Massachusetts Bay colony to challenge the Puritan leadership. The Puritan clergy had announced their intention to "reduce to obedience" all they could reach. The Society of Friends launched a frontal assault on Puritanism. They burst into churches and lectured ministers. During services they shattered empty bottles to illustrate the spiritual emptiness of sermons.

The Puritans claimed the Devil had unleashed a "pernicious set of Heretics." Quakers were whipped, branded, or driven from town. Those stubborn enough to return had their tongues bored with hot pokers. Quaker children were sold as slaves in the West Indies. Before the Puritan violence ended, six people—one woman and five men—were executed.

The Society of Friends finally settled on Pennsylvania land that Quaker convert William Penn had negotiated for in a 1682 treaty with the Iroquois. Penn's tolerant society welcomed ethnic and religious minorities. Welsh, Germans, Quakers, and Jews lived at peace with one another and their Iroquois neighbors.

Swedes, who arrived in Wilmington, Delaware, in 1638 on two ships launched by the Swedish West India Company, faced a different problem. To honor their youthful queen, they first named their settlement Fort Christina and then developed a brisk business of trading fur and tobacco. Delaware was soon in competition with nearby Dutch and English colonies. In 1655 Governor Stuyvesant sent his fleet and, without firing a shot, it captured and annexed Delaware's New Sweden.

By then Swedish log cabins, with traditional low doors and loophole windows, housed an ethnically diverse population. Welcome was extended to army deserters, debtors, and minor criminals. Johan Printz, the 300-pound Governor, had only one complaint—there were not enough "true Christians."

This was not a minor problem for Swedish Americans. At the end of the seventeenth century a thousand residents of Delaware

Quakers being whipped in Massachusetts.

signed requests for Swedish pastors. The mother country finally sent three ministers as well as a collection of Swedish Bibles and hymn books.

But New Sweden had changed. In 1730 preachers had to give three sermons—in Swedish, English, and German. Swedes had become assimilated with other Americans. This caused complaints. In 1745 Reverend Abraham Reincke wrote:

I found in this country scarcely one genuine Swede left, the most of them are part or in whole on one side or the other descended from English or Dutch parents, some of them have a Dutch, German, or English father, others a Swedish mother, and others a Dutch or English mother and a Swedish father. Many of them can just recollect that their grandfathers or mothers were Swedish . . . . The English are evidently swallowing up the people, and the Swedish language is so corrupted, that if I did not know the English, it would be impossible to understand the language of my own dear Sweden.

This fear of assimilation was echoed by every ethnic and religious minority who reached these shores. French Canadian Catholics in English colonies or territories also had to resist pressure to assimilate with the Protestant majority. The French Catholics tenaciously held to their customs and religion. These French people had first ventured into the Ohio valley as fur trappers. Others came to New England during the Revolution preferring American to British rule. Some settled on or near Lake Champlain, and others in Vincennes, Indiana, and Kankakee, Illinois. After the Revolution other French Canadians migrated to the Great Lakes and Maine. They brought an unshakable faith in Catholicism. By keeping their mother tongue, they felt they had fortified their devotion to family, faith, and tradition.

French Acadians, driven from Canada, settled in what is now Illinois and Louisiana.

French Canadian pathfinders entered the Louisiana Territory as well. In 1796 Julien Dubuque founded Dubuque, Iowa. In 1812 Joseph Robidon began St. Joseph, Missouri. And in 1818 Laurent Juneau founded Milwaukee. By 1820 more than 4,000 French Canadians immigrants had crowded into the bustling frontier town of Detroit.

Nevertheless, prejudice against Catholics remained strong in the English colonies. "Papists," as Catholics were sometimes called because they were led by the Pope, were denied rights, and priests were not welcome.

Catholics gained political power in Maryland under Lord Baltimore, and they passed a Toleration Act in 1649. It extended religious protection to Catholics and other Christians. Excluded from its provisions were Unitarians, Jews, Quakers, and atheists. These people would have to wait longer to gain their religious liberty in Maryland.

But groups opposed to Catholicism regained power in Maryland. In 1690 a new law required the imprisonment of any priest who entered the colony. If he escaped, he faced the death penalty. A citizen who harbored a priest faced three days standing in the pillory.

Jacob Leisler, Immigrant and Rebel

Born in Frankfurt, Germany, in 1640, at age 20 Jacob Leisler sailed to British America and settled in New York. In 1689 he led armed New Yorkers against a royal governor who represented wealthy landlords and merchants and who exercised arbitrary power in the colony. Royal officials fled and the government fell into the hands of Leisler's band of middle-class storekeepers and merchants.

During the two years of Leisler's rules he brought tax and other reforms. He promoted self-government and initiated New York's first elected assembly.

Although Leisler swore his loyalty to King William, the king found his reforms too radical to tolerate. William appointed Colonel Henry Sloughter governor of New York and sent him with enough troops to crush Leisler's government and arrest him.

Leisler was sentenced to the gallows. He appealed to the king for clemency, but before clemency could be granted, Leisler's enemies saw that the death sentence was carried out. Leisler died, but his New York Assembly lived on. Parliament soon restored Leisler's estate to his heirs. Later the New York Assembly voted his heirs an apology and a cash settlement. Leisler had begun his revolution a century too soon. In the end his deeds were no longer considered crimes and his ideas inspired many other Americans also bent on revolution. ■

One large group of Catholics in America were the Irish. Ireland itself had long been ruled by Protestant England, but most of the Irish had remained Catholic. There were Protestant Irish in the northern part of Ireland, and members of both groups, Protestants and Catholics, settled in America. Trinity Church in New York had 95 Irish graves by the year 1800, and St. Paul's Church in the same city had 62. On St. Patrick's Day in 1737, 26 Irish members of Boston's Presbyterian church formed an Irish Society.

The Catholic and Protestant Irish animosity did not entirely change in the New World. Irish Protestants in Londonderry, New Hampshire, announced, "We were surprised to hear ourselves termed Irish people, when we so frequently ventured our all for the British Crown and Liberties against the Irish Papists."

But some British colonists expressed disdain of all Irish. A Boston official claimed, "These confounded Irish will eat us up, provisions being most extravagantly dear, and scarce . . . ." Although the Irish contributed their labor to the hardest jobs and were paid the smallest salaries, they were often resented for their poverty.

Ethnic rivalry could become violent. In Winchester, Virginia, Irish and Dutch citizens taunted each other. On St. Patrick's Day the Dutch built an effigy of a Catholic saint decorated with Irish potatoes. Rioting followed. On the Dutch St. Michael's Day the Irish retaliated with an effigy of the saint with a necklace of sauerkraut, and rioting again followed. Virginia courts finally punished enough rioters to halt the taunts and mayhem. Eventually peace reigned in Winchester.

Despite its old and new obstacles, the New World spelled opportunity. Immigrant men and women found success hard but not impossible. Almost any free person who worked hard and saved money might become a landowner. Many did.

In the New World, colonial leaders could arise from every economic class. Aristocrats did not always win, and the poor did not always lose. A few sought great wealth, and some found it.

But most settlers were content to pursue the security that comes with land ownership. Intrepid pioneers tramped into the wilderness to carve out their dream of a home and some land. They had left a continent that offered no such chance. On American soil, European men and women found far greater opportunities for security and advancement than they had back home.

An old poster inviting Germans to emigrate to North America.

CHAPTER 12

WOMEN POETS

Though denied social and economic equality, colonial women grasped for means of self-expression. A few found it in poetry.

Anne Bradstreet was married at 16, and two years later, in 1630, she and her husband left England for Puritan Massachusetts. She became the daughter of one Massachusetts governor and the wife of another. She had three children and began writing poetry. Without her knowledge, her brother-in-law had her poetry published. As the first woman author in the British colonies, she suddenly became famous. One of her verses provides a candid view of how some men treated her as a poet and woman:

> I am obnoxious to each carping tongue
> Who says my hand a needle better fits,
> A poet's pen all scorn I should thus wrong,
> For such despite they cast on female wits:
> If what I do prove well, it won't advance,
> They'll say it's stolen, or else it was by chance.

In 1735 Lucy Terry was 5 years old when she was kidnapped from Africa and sold as a slave in Deerfield, Massachusetts. When a battle with Native Americans erupted at her village in 1746, Terry, then 16, wrote of the event in rhyme. Her poem was considered to be the best depiction of the event recorded. It was also the first poem in the Americas written by an African woman.

Lucy Terry married Abijah Prince, a free African 25 years older than she, and a founder of Sunderland, Vermont. He bought her freedom, and the couple raised a family. Two of their sons volunteered in the American Revolution and returned safely. Events then thrust Terry into legal confrontations. When a neighbor tore down her fences and set her haystacks ablaze, she carried her fury and objections to the Vermont Governor's Council. It ruled in her favor. When her youngest son was denied admission to Williams College,

Terry lectured the trustees for three hours about their obligation to accept students on an equal basis. She argued in vain.

A boundary dispute with a neighbor in Sunderland, Vermont, again brought Lucy Terry to court. This time she argued her case against one of Vermont's best lawyers and won. The judge told the court that she had made a better argument than he "had heard from any lawyer at the Vermont bar."

Phillis Wheatley, at 9 was also kidnapped from Africa and sold as a slave in Boston. A Quaker family taught the frail young girl to read and encouraged her writing talents. Her first book of verses was published in 1773. It was the second volume of poetry to be published by an American woman. Her works drew praise from Voltaire, John Hancock, Benjamin Franklin, and George Washington. She was devoted to the cause of American independence and published a poem extolling George Washington for his leadership of the patriot army. Washington wrote and asked her to visit him, and the two met at his Cambridge headquarters. No one recorded what the poet and the general said to each other about liberty or poetry.

Phillis Wheatley, a poet of the Revolutionary War.

CHAPTER 13

PONTIAC'S RISING

Peace in the Americas was often interrupted by European gunfire. As foreign nations battled over land, they also hired Native Americans as troops. In order to rid their land of one European enemy, Indian nations felt they had to fight for another. But each war only led to others.

In 1763 after seven years of warfare, the British defeated France and forced it to surrender the Ohio valley and Canada. This ended a series of European wars in British America.

However, ten Native American nations saw the Ohio valley as their homeland, and they had no intention of surrendering it. Pontiac, who commanded the Pawnees and the loyalty of dozens of Native American societies, told the British:

> Englishmen, although you have conquered the French,
> you have not yet conquered us. We are not your slaves.
> These lakes, these woods, and mountains were left us by
> our ancestors. They are our inheritance; and we will part
> with them to none.

He began to warn his people against adopting the ways of Europeans, particularly their firearms and liquor. These, he said, made Native Americans weak and dependent. For his people to gain enough strength to defeat the invaders, he insisted, they must unite and return to ancient traditions. Pontiac explained:

> My children, you have forgotten the customs and traditions
> of your forefathers. Why do you not clothe yourselves in
> skins, as they did, use bows and arrows and the stone-
> pointed lances, which they used? You have bought guns,
> knives, kettles, and blankets from the white man until you
> can no longer do without them; and what is worse you have
> drunk the poison firewater, which turns you into fools. Fling
> all these things away; live as your forefathers did before you.

Mounting support from other Indian nations encouraged Pontiac to strike at British forts in the Ohio valley. A white Detroit resident reported what he thought the British feared most: "The Indians are saving and caressing all the Negroes they take," and this might "produce an insurrection."

But Pontiac's plans did not include appeals to Africans. His lightning raids caught the British off guard, and within weeks Pontiac's forces had captured eight forts. For Sir Jeffrey Amherst, commander of British North American forces, shock turned to rage, and he proposed a final solution to his Indian problem. Amherst recommended to his assistant, Colonel Henry Bouquet, that he

A 19th century European print of Chief Pontiac's meeting with British officers.

"send the smallpox" into Pontiac's villages. He suggested infected blankets should be used. Bouquet obeyed his orders.

Bouquet also said he wished to train savage dogs to track and destroy "that vermin." General Amherst approved the idea and urged the colonel to continue to think creatively about "every method" to exterminate "this execrable race." He added, "I wish to hear of no prisoners." A smallpox epidemic was soon raging among Pontiac's people.

A few months later, 57 residents of Paxton, Pennsylvania, calling themselves "the Paxton boys," destroyed a peaceful Conestoga Indian village and murdered the people they found—three Indian men, two women, and a boy. Until then, whites had always considered the Conestogas to be a friendly people.

The governor placed the surviving Conestogas under his protection at the Lancaster jail. Then this "Paxton mob" marched on Lancaster, broke into the prison, and killed the captives.

The genocide policy advocated by Amherst and carried out by Bouquet and the Paxton mob often was rooted in economic gain. This was made clear in a play written by Robert Rogers, who commanded Rogers' Rangers against Pontiac in the Ohio valley. Rogers' play called Indians "savage beasts" and "cursed infidels" who "don't deserve to breathe in Christian air and should be hunted down like other brutes." Rogers' point was that Indians "kidnap all the game" at a moment when trapping and hunting in the Ohio valley offered Europeans large financial rewards.

CHAPTER 14

THE DECLARATION OF INDEPENDENCE

The Declaration of Independence was the world's first and loudest call for liberty and justice based on natural rights. Though it was born in the struggle to overturn British colonial rule, it became a document for freedom fighters of other ages.

Its author, Thomas Jefferson, had not originated its main ideas but learned them elsewhere. The Declaration's ideas came from John Locke, an English philosopher, Charles Lucas, an Irish revolutionary, Cesare Beccaria, an Italian economist, Emmerich Von Vattel, a Swiss jurist, Charles Louis de Montesquieu, a French philosopher, and Samuel von Pufendorf, a German historian.

The Declaration's language was anticipated by the writings of Thomas Paine, a Quaker radical who emigrated from England to America in 1774. Early in 1776 Paine's *Common Sense* became the inspiration for independence. "It worked a powerful change in the minds of many men," wrote George Washington.

Later that year Paine's series of pamphlets called *The Crisis* was printed by Charles Cist, a Russian immigrant. By then, Paine at 40, followed his own advice and had volunteered as a common soldier in the Continental Army.

Jefferson was also influenced by his Virginia neighbor, Philip Mazzei, an Italian doctor. In Tuscany, Italy, Mazzei had battled the Inquisition which charged him with having dangerous books. Jefferson brought him to Virginia and granted him vast acreage next to his Monticello home. He invested heavily in Mazzei's project to develop Italian silkworms, olives, and wine grapes. Jefferson translated an article Mazzei wrote in Italian in 1774. He borrowed from its profound words: "All men are by nature created free and independent . . . . Every individual must be equal to every other in his natural rights." The two discussed political matters and Jefferson

Thomas Paine, an English Quaker, took a leading part in the American and French revolutions.

introduced Mazzei to other Virginians such as Patrick Henry, James Madison, and George Washington. Governor Patrick Henry later sent Mazzei to Europe to raise money for the independence cause.

The Declaration had eloquently justified resistance to tyranny. But decades before Jefferson's words, Native Americans and Africans had also battled European tyrants and slaveholders in the Americas. Slave rebels acted on the idea that all human beings had a natural right to freedom and a right to resist unjust authority. Before Patrick Henry said "Give me liberty or give me death!" Africans and Indians had shed their blood for freedom. African men and women battled against a despotism more ruthlessly cruel than any King George III had imposed on the 13 colonies. Native Americans had to confront a British policy of genocide toward their villagers.

At the Boston Massacre of 1770, Crispus Attucks, a Black Natick Indian, was the first to die for American independence.

The fight for liberty came when every fifth American was in chains. This added an ironic dimension to the War for Independence. Some slaveholders and Indian fighters who now fought for independence from England, gained their first military experience against Native Americans defending their land.

The American Revolution lived with its inconsistencies. In 1765 the Sons of Liberty paraded in Charleston chanting "Liberty." A few months later African American slaves marched for freedom in these same streets. For a week armed whites scoured the nearby countryside searching for these dangerous rebels.

However, not all Americans ignored the contradiction between slavery and the fight for liberty. In 1774 Abigail Adams wrote her husband John of a slave plot for liberty. To the man who sat on Jefferson's committee to draft the Declaration, she offered her opinion: "It always appeared a most iniquitous scheme to me to fight for ourselves for what we are daily robbing and plundering from those who have as good a right to freedom as we have."

From the earliest days of colonial unrest, Africans hoped to find their own liberty in the struggle against British colonialism. On a snowy night in March 1770, a black Natick Indian and a runaway slave named Crispus Attucks stepped into history. As a leader of patriots in what became the "Boston Massacre," he became the first to die for American independence. Among others present that fateful night were some Irish seamen and at least one other African American.

Black voices began to use phrases about natural rights coined by the patriots. In 1773 African Americans in Massachusetts petitioned for freedom and "no taxation without representation." Others battled for freedom without relying on words. A month before Minutemen bravely stood at Concord bridge, slaves in Ulster County, New York, organized a revolt against their masters. Some 500 Indians were also said to have been involved in their massive plot.

When Paul Revere galloped off to warn the minutemen that the British were coming, he rode into history. But so did others. In Connecticut, Sybil Luddington, at 16, galloped twice as many miles to warn twice as many minutemen as did Revere. The forces Luddington rallied recaptured valuable supplies British troops had seized. In South Carolina, Francis Salvador, a Portuguese Jew, raced

The Abigail Adams Letters

On March 31, 1776, Abigail Adams wrote to her husband, John Adams. She wanted to remind him of the rights of women since he was on the committee charged with writing the Declaration of Independence.

> I desire you would remember the ladies and be more generous and favorable to them than your ancestors. Do not put such unlimited power into the hands of the husbands. Remember, all men would be tyrants if they could. If particular care and attention is not paid to the ladies, we are determined to foment a rebellion, and will not hold ourselves bound by any laws in which we have no voice or representation.

She wrote again on May 7, 1776:

> I cannot say that I think you are very generous to the ladies; for whilst you are proclaiming peace and good will to men . . . you insist on retaining an absolute power over wives. But you must remember that arbitrary power is like most other things which are very hard, very liable to be broken; and not withstanding all your wise laws and maxims, we have it in our power, not only to free ourselves but to subdue our masters . . . . ■

his steed 28 miles to warn patriots the British were coming. His gravestone carried this proud epitaph:

> True to his ancient faith, he gave his life for new hopes of human liberty and understanding.

In April 1775, among the minutemen who returned British fire at Lexington and Concord were Irish Americans and African Americans. Paradoxically, that summer, patriots from Maryland to Georgia were fighting slave rebels. In three North Carolina counties alone hundreds of slaves clashed with their former owners.

The slavery issue actually altered the phrasing in the Declaration of Independence. In the document's first draft, Jefferson denounced King George III for promoting slavery and the slave trade. But pro-slavery delegates then demanded its elimination, and it was removed from the final version.

On July 4, 1776, John Hancock put his bold scrawl across the Declaration of Independence. Maryland's Charles Carroll, an Irish Catholic and the wealthiest delegate to the Continental Congress was among the 56 signers. Four immigrants from Ireland and five others of Irish descent signed. Scots James Wilson and John Witherspoon and three Ulster Scots also signed the Declaration. Another signer was William Pica, an Italian who would serve as governor of Maryland from 1782 to 1786. Pica is also claimed by the Portuguese and Czechs as one of their own. John Morton, whose grandfather was an original settler of New Sweden, Delaware, also signed the document. The Continental Congress' printer, Johan Treutlen, a German or Austrian immigrant, was the first to publish the historic document in his Philadelphia *Staatsbote*.

The slaves' zeal for liberty seemed to rise during the fight for American independence. On July 5th John Hancock received a letter telling how slaves in New Jersey had seized arms to battle for freedom. In the seven years of war between 1776 and 1783 an estimated 100,000 men, women, and children escaped from slavery. Jefferson estimated that 30,000 had fled their chains in 1778 alone.

To defeat the powerful British army, the Continental Congress depended on unity among its diverse population. They found it particularly strong among Irish Americans who identified with this struggle to wrench free of British authority because of the same struggle in their homeland. The Continental Congress boasted 22 men of Irish ancestry or birth. In 1771 Philadelphia's Friendly Sons of St. Patrick began to supply the patriots with gifts of money.

In the Mohawk Valley, the patriot cause found allies among German farmers arrayed against British landlords. In 1774 these Germans issued their own statement of independence, and by the next year they formed a revolutionary committee. Under their chosen general, Nicholas Herkimer, they recruited four battalions for the Continental Army. A dynamic German preacher, Reverend John Peter Muhlenberg, urged fellow citizens to enlist. In January 1776, he told his Pennsylvania congregation: "There is a time for preaching and praying, but there is also a time for battle, and that time has now arrived." Then he threw off his clerical robes and revealed the blue and gold uniform of a colonel in the Continental Army. The Continental Congress desperately needed such spirited, patriotic fighters.

When Continental troops invaded Quebec in 1775, they found French Canadians who welcomed them as liberators. Two of these, Moses Hazen and James Livingston, recruited 500 men in two companies to assist the Americans. By the time the American forces left Canada, more than 100 French Canadians marched in their ranks. This began a long identification between freedom fighters in Canada and the United States.

Reverend John Muhlenberg revealing his Continental Army uniform to his German American congregation in Pennsylvania.

Inspired by the Declaration's stirring words of hope, the colonists had dared to break from the British Crown. But now they had to face in the British army and navy, the strongest armed forces of the day.

Early skirmishes brought out more than minutemen with their muskets. On the battlefield many colonists found a sense of purpose and pride, a common nationality and destiny. To achieve victory, many kinds of people had to become a unified force.

The patriot cause had depended on the determination, resourcefulness, and raw courage of many such as Crispus Attucks, Sybil Luddington, Moses Hazen, Peter Muhlenberg, Thomas Paine, and Charles Carroll. The revolution's success would rest on many thousands of such daring volunteers, a host of foreigners, and distant allies.

CHAPTER 15

THE VICTORIOUS REVOLUTION

The Continental Army eagerly recruited soldiers regardless of their ability to speak English. Citizens and immigrants, those who spoke in foreign accents, and Catholics, Protestants, and Jews all were signed up.

About 141 Hungarian Americans served as soldiers for General George Washington's army. At the Battle of Monmouth, in New Jersey, in 1778, an American soldier named Ypsilantis led other Greek Americans into battle. So many Irish Americans served that some British politicians claimed that the North American colonies had fallen to an Irish army.

In Carlisle, Pennsylvania, seven of the first nine American companies formed were mostly Irish American, and two were largely German American. In Charleston, South Carolina, 26 Jewish Americans who lived on King Street enlisted at the same time in "The Jews' Company." Under General William Moultrie, they fought in the Battle of Beaufort. When Rhode Island did not meet its quota of soldiers, Colonel Christopher Greene was dispatched to find more by General Washington. He recruited a regiment of 93 ex-slaves and 30 free African American volunteers.

The Continentals desperately needed brave men such as Nathan Hale who was executed as a spy by the British. Another brave man was Mordecai Sheftall. When the British captured Savannah, they jailed this Jewish director of Georgia's patriotic revolutionary brigade. Sheftall steadfastly refused to divulge any information to the enemy and then escaped to Philadelphia.

In 1778 Giuseppe Vigo, an Italian, guided Captain George Rogers Clark's army 250 miles to capture Vincennes, Indiana. Vigo then was able to convince local Native Americans to remain neutral and to persuade Clark's French soldiers to accept the worthless

Virginia currency as pay. By swallowing a document before his captors could question him, Vigo avoided execution as a spy.

The war sometimes divided families. Though General Nicholas Herkimer organized four battalions among his fellow German Americans, his brother remained a Tory officer. Isaac and David Franks were Jewish brothers who became high ranking American officers, but their older cousin remained a staunch loyalist.

During the terrible winter at Valley Forge, local German American farmers provided food for Washington's ragged troops. Some German Americans and Moravians served as nurses. Others, as convinced pacifists, refused to fight for either side. After the Battle of Brandywine, these pacifists volunteered to staff a hospital for the Continental casualties.

Some enemies turned into friends and allies. German princes hired out 29,875 Hessians as mercenaries to the British. In Germany, one third failed to appear for muster. Those who crossed the Atlantic showed little taste for dying for the British Crown. Many surrendered to the Americans. After some Hessian captives were taken on a tour of Pennsylvania's rich farmlands, almost all volunteered to remain. One was Private Kuster, an ancestor of the dashing General George Armstrong Custer.

The Irish provided about 1,500 officers, including 26 generals, more than half born in Ireland. Two regiments of French forces arrayed against the British were actually composed of Irishmen. Three Irish American officers made significant contributions to the patriot cause. John Barry was the first commissioned navy captain. General John Sullivan had served in the Continental Congress before the war. He served in many battles and with Washington at Valley Forge. Irish Andrew Lewis had been recommended by Washington to be Commander-in-Chief of the Continental Army. One of Washington's most trusted officers was Christian Febiger, a Dane. Another was General Johann Kalb, a giant of a man from Germany, who served under General Horatio Gates.

Benjamin Nones, a French Jew, enlisted as a private, was cited for bravery, and became a major under Generals Washington and Lafayette. Haym Salomon, a Jewish immigrant from Poland began a revolutionary career serving as a member of the Sons of Liberty. In the Revolution he was arrested as a spy in New York. After fleeing captivity, he helped French and American prisoners escape from the British. Salomon was a wealthy man who raised about $200,000 for the Revolution and endorsed the valueless currency issued by the Continental Congress. He died a pauper. Giuseppe Vigo spent his fortune of $8,616 for independence and also died poor.

From the outset of the revolution, African American volunteers early posed a dilemma in an army led by slaveholders. George Washington first opposed recruitment of slaves. Then in November 1775, British governor Lord Dunmore issued a proclamation offering freedom and a musket to any slave who reached his lines. "The flame runs like a wildfire through the slaves," wrote a white women.

The patriots had to act quickly. The next month Washington asked and Congress authorized black enlistments. About 8,000 African Americans served in George Washington's army and John Paul Jones' navy. They helped capture Fort Ticonderoga with Ethan Allen's Green Mountain boys, crossed the Delaware with Washington, and lined up at Yorktown to receive the British surrender. "No regiment is to be seen in which there are not negroes in abundance," reported a Hessian soldier.

At Bunker Hill, African American Peter Salem shot the British commander, and another, Salem Poor, was cited for battlefield gallantry by Captain William Prescott and 13 of his officers.

Peter Salem kills British Major Pitcairn at Bunker Hill.

In the Carolinas, "Swamp Fox" Francis Marion led a band that included whites and Blacks. James Armistead, a slave, served as a spy for French general Marquis de Lafayette. Later General Lafayette saw that Armistead was given his freedom as a reward for his daring acts.

Women also played a vital role in many aspects of the war. In 1777 Lydia Darragh, a Quaker, let British officers meet in her Philadelphia home. She pretended to be asleep and listened as they planned a surprise attack. The next day she reported their strategy to an American officer, and the attack was foiled.

Women accompanied their soldier husbands to the front. Some volunteered as cooks, nurses, and launderers for the army. In 1776 Molly Corbin replaced a wounded man and loaded a cannon until she was wounded. Mary Ludwig, a German married to John Hays, carried water to the patriots under fire in 1778 during the Battle of Monmouth. The men named her Molly Pitcher. When Hays was wounded, she took over his job and manned a cannon. For her heroism, General Washington made Pitcher a sergeant and gave her officer's pay.

Deborah Sampson disguised herself as a man to enlist as Robert Shurtleff. She fought in several battles. When she was wounded, a doctor finally discovered she was a woman. She was honorably discharged with a pension of $8 a month.

Without foreign help, the Revolution might have failed. Spain, France, and Holland also saw England as the foe and deployed their forces against the British at sea and on land. Soldiers and sailors from Spain, Cuba, France, Mexico, and Puerto Rico, helped defeat Great Britain. Most of Ireland was on the side of the Americans. From California to Cuba, Spanish men and women aided the patriot cause. The governor of Louisiana, Bernardo de Galvez, sent food, guns, and medicine to American armies on the frontier. Cuban governor Juan Manuel de Cagigal, his assistant Francisco de Miranda, and many enterprising Cuban women raised money for Washington and the French forces during the campaign at Yorktown.

The Marquis de Lafayette was only one foreign aristocrat who played a vital part in the American victory. At Valley Forge, German General Friedrich von Steuben, who could not speak any English, drilled a disheartened, freezing army. His words had to be translat-

Deborah Sampson dressed as male soldier Robert Shurtleff.

Baron von Steuben brought drill and order to the Continental Army at Valley Forge.

ed from German to French and then to English. But soldiers standing in the snow learned discipline and had courage breathed into their hearts. Von Steuben's knowledge of siege tactics, unsurpassed in the war, were vital to the final victory at Yorktown.

There were other valuable and courageous Continental army officers from Europe. Major Cosmo Medici of Italy survived 41 months of battles and eleven months as a prisoner of war. Thaddeus Kosciusko, a Polish engineer, became a friend of Washington and Jefferson and a leading war hero. In 1777 he built the fortifications that led to the crucial victory at Saratoga. After this battle, France recognized the new American government and agreed to provide it full military and economic assistance. In 1783 Kosciusko was made a general. He returned home to marshal his own people against Russian tyrants.

In 1777 Polish count Casimir Pulaski saved the patriot forces at Brandywine. He then formed a Pulaski Legion largely staffed by Polish, German, and French officers. Pulaski later became the father of the American cavalry. His major training officer was Colonel Michael Kovats, a Hungarian, appointed by General Washington. Kovats' soldiers were mostly German Americans with some Hungarians. In 1779 Pulaski and Kovats died leading their men in Georgia.

St. Patrick's Day at Valley Forge

At Valley Forge in 1780 George Washington's bedraggled army huddled over its winter campfires. There were so many young Irish American soldiers that they decided they wanted to celebrate St. Patrick's Day.

General Washington was dubious, but because the men were persistent, he finally agreed. Washington did request that the Irish be sure "that the celebration of the Day will not be attended with the least Rioting and Disorder." He had heard about the Irish reputation for fighting and wanted their energies confined to battles against the British. ■

During the siege of Savannah, 700 black Haitian troops helped stem a British assault that could have wiped out the Americans. Among the wounded was Henri Christophe, a young black slave born in 1767. He returned home, and with Toussaint L'Ouverture, led the revolt that ended European rule and human slavery on their Caribbean island. In 1811 Christophe became King Henri of Haiti.

Soldiers of simple backgrounds showed unusual valor. Peter Francisco, huge at 16, was a Portuguese American in the 10th Virginia Regiment. He slew eleven men with his sword. He also captured a cannon, turned it around, and fired at the British. Oliver Cromwell, a black soldier who crossed the Delaware in Washington's boat, went on to survive the battles at Princeton, Brandywine, Monmouth, and Yorktown.

Polish count Casimir Pulaski, hero of the Revolution, died leading a cavalry charge in Georgia.

The Continental Congress also urged shipowners to arm and deploy as "privateers" against the British navy. Lithuanian Feliks Milaszevicz of Boston was one who armed his *Scotch Trick* and *Prince Radvil* for raids against the enemy at sea.

When the British finally surrendered at Yorktown in 1781, Lord Cornwallis' band played "The World Turned Upside Down." It probably seemed that way to Cornwallis and his aristocratic officers. The world's most powerful empire had been soundly defeated by a ragged band of colonists of every color, language, and nationality.

Some colonists who had remained loyal to England left with the British troops for Canada, the Bahamas, or England. The defeated also took many ex-slaves who had joined their ranks seeking liberty. More than 3,000 left from New York alone. Some were sold in the West Indies, but others found the freedom they longed for in Canada or elsewhere in the British Empire.

In Pennsylvania and the lower Hudson valley Hessian soldiers stayed on. In the Minisink Indian nation they intermarried with the Africans and Native Americans. Along the lower Hudson River these people of color began to call themselves the Ramapos.

The war for independence brought a new recognition to patriots who were not British. Of the thirteen states, nine had governors who were born in Scotland or had ancestors from Ireland or Scotland. In 1781 under the Articles of Confederation, the first American chief executive was Maryland's John Hanson, a Swedish American. George Washington called him the first president of the United States. Georgia elected as its first governor, Johann Treutlen, an Austrian or German. In 1801 Georgia elected as its governor Jewish war hero David Emmanuel who had distinguished himself at the Battle of Savannah.

The American Revolution demonstrated that American women and men of every color and national background were ready to die for liberty. But the struggle for freedom had just begun.

Many Americans still lived in chains. The poor could not vote, and women did not have equal rights. But daring American patriots had defeated British despotism and proudly launched their own representative government. For this reason, the American Revolution forever shone as a beacon for the oppressed of the world. A democratic spirit began to radiate from the former thirteen British colonies.

CHAPTER 16

A CONSTITUTION FOR A NEW NATION

The 55 men who drew up the U.S. Constitution in 1787 knew that more than white Englishmen had fought and died for American independence. They also knew the world's first republican experiment in government could survive only if its people remained unified.

To avoid discord, the new Constitution mentioned no deity and imposed no religious test for holding office. Thomas Fitzsimons, an Irish Catholic merchant in Philadelphia, was among the signers. (By contrast Catholics were barred from the British House of Commons until 1829, Jews until 1858, and atheists for another generation.)

The new United States opened up an era of religious diversity. In 1788 when thousands paraded in Philadelphia to celebrate the Constitution's ratification, Rabbi Gershom Sexias of the Hope of Israel Synagogue marched between two Christian ministers. Two years later President Washington wrote a warm letter to the Jewish congregation in Newport, Rhode Island. He pledged to give "to bigotry no sanction, to persecution no assistance." To Irish Catholics he also penned a similarly warm, appreciative letter.

Irish immigrant Thomas Kennedy introduced a bill in Maryland's legislature to provide equal rights to Jews. He had never met a Jew, he said, and simple justice was the issue. For years he campaigned for his bill, but success did not come until 1826. Until then some states still carried restrictive laws. In New York Catholics could not become citizens. Only Christians could vote, or hold office in Pennsylvania. In Delaware non-Christians could vote but only Christians could be elected. The Georgia legislature admitted only Protestants, and North Carolina and New Jersey allowed only Protestants to hold office.

Some English-speaking Americans made rapid progress.

Americans with Scottish backgrounds were three of the first U.S. Supreme Court judges. Of the thirteen new states, nine elected men with Scottish backgrounds as governors, including New York's George Clinton, seven times elected governor and twice elected vice president of the United States. Most German Americans showed little interest in politics, but some also made strides. The Muhlenberg family sent two members to the first U.S. Congress where Frederick became the first Speaker of the House and was twice reelected. He had the honor of signing the Bill of Rights with Vice President John Adams. In 1791 John Kittera, a descendant of the Moravian Brethren, was elected to Congress and served two terms. Michael Hilligas, a German Huguenot American, became the first U.S. treasurer.

The Constitution granted neither citizenship nor protection to Native Americans or Africans. Its rights and privileges were reserved for whites.

At the Constitutional Convention slavery was the unresolved issue. When a delegate said that slaves were no different than sheep, Benjamin Franklin asked him when was the last time anyone heard of sheep leading an insurrection.

The authors of the Constitution tried mightily to reach a compromise on the slavery issue. First, the document did not mention the word "slave." But bondage was dealt with in three separate sections. The document called for an end to the slave trade in 20 years.

The Constitution and a New Church

One Sunday in November 1786, Reverends Richard Allen, Absolom Jones, and other black worshipers in Philadelphia took their seats at St. George's Methodist Episcopal Church. Then a white trustee told them to move to seats in the upstairs gallery.

They reached the gallery and got on their knees to pray. Suddenly, trustees tried to pull them to their feet. A scuffle broke out as Allen, Jones, and the others shoved the trustees away. The black men completed their prayers and left in a body.

The next year, as white delegates in Philadelphia wrote a new Constitution, Jones and Allen formed the Free African Society. It soon gave birth to the first African American church. They had asserted their right to religious liberty, but had found themselves unable to do this with white Americans in the new republic. ■

It also provided for the return of fugitive slaves. It counted each slave as three-fifths of a person for purposes of taxes and votes. This gave additional votes to slave owners. It also seemed to state that whites believed that Blacks were lesser humans.

Many delegates thought that slavery was dying and that their compromises were necessary to unite the country. They did not mean to extend the life of a system most of them strongly opposed.

Some may have seen the Constitution as sealing the fate of slavery. Since it called for an end to importing Africans as slaves, this would soon dry up slavery's source. The Northwest Ordinance in that same year of 1787 banned slavery in the Ohio valley. Northern states also had begun to emancipate their slaves. These two actions appeared to doom bondage in the North and West. Many delegates to the Constitutional Convention believed that the slave system had suffered mortal blows and could not survive for very long.

The invention of the cotton gin made slavery a very profitable system for cotton plantation owners.

Events proved otherwise. The invention of the cotton gin in 1793 turned slavery into a profitable southern system. One slave at a machine could pick out the seeds that previously took the efforts of 50 slaves. Cotton became a popular crop as more fields spread westward to Mississippi, Alabama, and Arkansas.

The slave trade was banned by Congress in 1808—but traders routinely violated it. Human bondage in America did not die. Instead, it began to tear the new nation in half.

Women were also disappointed by the new government. Every day they proved their equal worth, especially as patriots during the war. But under the law they had no more rights than children. The law considered them to be wards of their husbands or fathers.

Viewed by today's standards, the Constitution had created a republic for the few, not the many. The Constitution may have been a flawed and incomplete document. However, it insured democratic progress in America. It created the most advanced republican government the world had ever seen. It accepted the revolutionary belief that political power rests with the people rather than a king or a privileged elite. Thomas Jefferson called the Constitution "a good canvas, on which some strokes only want retouching." He specifically talked of the need for a bill of rights. In two years the Bill of Rights, the first 10 amendments to the Constitution, was added. The rights of free speech, assembly, and petition, and the right to form political, religious, and other groups was protected by the Bill of Rights. Citizens were also protected from arbitrary searches and seizures, and in court proceedings from violations of their human rights.

The Bill of Rights and the Constitution gave Americans peaceful ways of reforming government and amending the Constitution. These were soon to be used to extend human rights. Additional amendments would protect people once excluded as citizens. The Founding Fathers said that the Constitution had created a "more perfect union." They understood that as time went on it would require changes, and they wanted these peacefully put in place.

CHAPTER 17

RIPPLES FROM THE AMERICAN REVOLUTION

The American Revolution and the words of the Declaration of Independence and Constitution were heard around the world. Among common people everywhere they struck a chord of deeply held democratic feelings. Above all, they invited other ordinary men and women to defy despotism. "We are pointing out the way to struggling nations who wish, like us, to emerge from their tyrannies also," wrote Thomas Jefferson.

From Ireland to Russia people learned that American men and women had stood up to the greatest military power on earth and won. Monarchs trembled to think that their subjects might follow in the footsteps of Washington and the minutemen. Few aristocrats were thrilled by the American victory, but in 1786 Morocco's Mohammed III signed a treaty of friendship with the Continental Congress. A year later, he became the first foreign head of state to recognize the independence of the United States.

Those who had come from distant lands to fight for independence returned home imbued with American ideals. Lafayette in France, Christophe in Haiti, and Kosciusko in Poland brought back enough courage and military experience to challenge their own tyrants. Francisco de Miranda returned to South America with an enthusiasm that fired one revolt after another against Spain. In France the American victory helped spark another revolution. In 1789 and the years following, the French stormed the Bastille, wrote a Declaration of the Rights of Man, and began a society dedicated to liberty and equality. Marching as a volunteer in their ranks was Thomas Paine, a voice of the American Revolution. In 1791 half a million free and enslaved Africans in Haiti led by Toussaint L'Ouverture and Henri Christophe launched the only successful land-based slave revolt in history. In 1801 Napoleon denounced the

Toussaint L'Ouverture confronts the enemy with his demands of independence for his people.

new Haitian Constitution for rejecting French colonial domination. L'Ouverture had a simple answer: "Why not? The United States did exactly that."

The democratic spirit, renewed by revolutionary fires in France and Haiti, warmed men and women all over the globe. In 1791 Poles wrote a Constitution modeled after the U.S. Constitution. In 1794 Kosciusko organized a peasant militia modeled in Poland after Washington's Army and led it against the Czar's despotic Russian Empire.

Meanwhile, the Revolution continued to move those at home. In 1800 in Henrico County, Virginia, slave Gabriel Prosser plotted to free his people in Richmond and the countryside around it. His plan was based on L'Ouverture's, and he carried a banner that read "Liberty or Death"—the slogan of Patrick Henry and of L'Ouverture.

Prosser intended to recruit Catawba Indians and to spare whites he believed were opposed to slavery, such as Quakers and

French people. He assembled 900 men to attack Richmond one night. But sudden storms washed out bridges and roads leading to the city. Drenched men returned home to await a new signal.

Then Virginia authorities uncovered the conspiracy and arrested the plotters. One of the captives told the Virginia court that condemned him:

> I have nothing more to offer than what George
> Washington would have had to offer had he been taken by
> the British and put to trial by them. I have ventured my
> life in endeavoring to obtain the liberty of my
> countrymen, and am a willing sacrifice to their cause.

The summer before the Constitutional delegates assembled, debt-ridden Massachusetts farmers rose in rebellion. War veterans Daniel Shays and Moses Sash, a free African American, tried to topple a political system that foreclosed on poor farmers and then jailed those who protested.

Shays' Rebellion freed fellow farmers from prison, but his armed forces were finally routed by the governor's troops. However, within a year the state's voters by a three to one majority drove the governor from office.

The Revolution had also given American women a proud, new view of themselves. First, they knew that many women had helped to defeat the British. In addition, on the frontier, they continued to share the perils and burdens of a dangerous life. Some, such as Abigail Adams, even began to understand that in a republic they did not have to accept an inferior citizenship.

African Americans also took heart from the victory over British rule. By 1790, 59,000 lived as free people in the 13 states. They knew fathers and uncles who had helped defeat the mighty British Empire. Beginning in 1780, Massachusetts Blacks, seeking to gain the vote, petitioned against "taxation without representation." Their protests spread to other states.

From distant lands and at home, many people of color and both sexes had seen ordinary people demonstrate their power during the Revolution. Now millions waited for their moment to say that human rights were inalienable and that all people should be free. Distant rulers shifted uneasily in their inherited thrones.

Revolutions in New Spain

During the American Revolution, Captain Francisco de Miranda, age 30, assisted General Juan de Cagigal, governor of Cuba, to capture Pensacola, Florida, and New Providence in the Bahamas from the British. As Miranda battled the English, he began to wonder if he might be able to end colonialism in South America.

Miranda participated in the French Revolution. Then, in 1806, he led fighters for freedom in Venezuela. In 1810, as independence fever seized his continent, he tried to become its first great liberator. Miranda was assisted by Venezuelan Símon Bólivar, 27, who had also visited the United States.

Latin American nations began to write their own declarations of independence: Venezuela and Paraguay in 1811, New Grenada (Colombia) and Mexico in 1813, the United Provinces of La Plata (Argentina) in 1816, Chile in 1818,

Vicente Guerrero, the black Indian president of Mexico in 1829.

Guatemala in 1823, and Uruguay and Bolivia in 1825. In 1819 at the Congress of Angostura, Bólivar was elected president of Venezuela and planned a strategy that would end colonial reign in the Americas. He urged unity across all ethnic and racial lines and spoke of a common history:

It is impossible to say to which human family we belong. The larger part of the Native population has disappeared. Europeans have mixed with the Indians and the Negroes, and Negroes have mixed with the Indians. We were all born of one mother America, though our fathers had different origins and we all have differently colored skins. This dissimilarity is of the greatest significance.

In Mexico, the independence struggle lasted into the 1820s. Many revolutionary leaders fell in battle or were captured. But Vicente Guerrero, born in 1782 to parents of African, Indian, and European blood, led his army of 2,000 to the Sierra Madre Mountains where the former mule driver trained his men.

In the mountains Guerrero, at 40, learned to read and write. By 1824 he helped shape the Mexican Constitution. By 1829 when he became president of Mexico, Spain had been defeated. President Guerrero ended slavery in his country. He has been called the George Washington and Abraham Lincoln of Mexico. ■

CHAPTER 18

TO STAND AGAINST SLAVERY

The American Revolution was not fought to end slavery, but it stimulated a movement by some whites to abolish or eliminate it. To patriots of conscience it seemed wrong to fight for inalienable rights while keeping Africans in chains. Some became strong abolitionists.

African Americans had demonstrated their equal abilities through their war service in the Continental or British Army. Some patriot leaders were also moved by slaves who led heroic rebellions, fled to the woods, joined Indian nations, or formed their own communities in the wilderness.

In 1688 the first white written antislavery protest was penned by Germantown, Pennsylvania, Quakers. What, they asked their fellow citizens, could be worse than being kidnapped and sold in a foreign land? How would whites like to be sent as "slaves to strange countries, separating husbands from their wives and children?" Africans have, stated the Quakers, "as much a right to fight for their freedom, as you have to keep them slaves."

Though not all Quakers were antislavery, some helped slave runaways and established schools for free people of color. In 1754 the most influential Quaker of the day, John Woolman, wrote a popular antislavery booklet arguing that African slaves "are the souls for whom Christ died."

The fight against British despotism breathed new fire into antislavery crusaders. Thomas Paine's first American pamphlet was not about independence but a condemnation of those who "enslave men by violence and murder for gain." He wrote, "No man can be happy surrounded by those whose happiness he has destroyed." Founding Fathers Benjamin Franklin, Alexander Hamilton, and James Otis favored emancipation. Dr. Benjamin Rush denounced profits made from "the sweat and blood of Negro slaves." He also

Benjamin Lay, the Quaker Conscience

A hunchback, four feet seven inches tall, with a large head and flowing red beard, Benjamin Lay frightened more people with his ideas than his looks. At 41 he left England for Barbados. For thirteen years he stirred resentment on the island just by practicing his religion and making friends with Africans and Natives.

By 1737, after Lay migrated to the thirteen colonies, he had written *All Slave-Keepers that Keep the Innocent in Bondage, Apostates*. His friend Benjamin Franklin published it. Quakers in Philadelphia expelled Lay for his bold attack on slavery. But he never stopped considering himself a Quaker. To convince his fellow Quakers to oppose bondage, Lay tried direct action. He stood barefoot in the snow before a Quaker meeting hall. When people showed concern, he said they ought to show concern for slaves whose conditions were far worse. Lay then kidnapped the child of a slaveholding family. He returned the child in a few days to the frantic parents. Can they now understand how slave parents feel? he asked.

Twenty years after the Quakers expelled Lay for his antislavery convictions, they voted to expel slaveholders. "Thanksgiving and praise be rendered unto the Lord God," Lay rejoiced, "I can now die in peace." He died the next year still believing that combating evil was more important than making friends. ■

Revolutionary hero Lafayette felt Americans next had to end slavery.

called for fair treatment of Native Americans, education of women, eliminating the death penalty, and urged greater public understanding of those people stricken with mental illnesses.

White antislavery societies were first organized during and after the Revolutionary War. Antislavery societies were organized in Rhode Island and New York in 1785, in Delaware in 1788, and in Maryland in 1789. Franklin became first president of the Pennsylvania antislavery society in 1789. By 1794, a national anti-slavery convention brought delegates from New Jersey, Delaware, Pennsylvania, New York, Maryland, Connecticut, and Virginia.

Lafayette was only one of the Revolution's foreign heroes who called for an end to slavery in the new republic. Kosciusko willed his money to free slaves. He asked Jefferson to see that some funds went to education, training, and whatever else would "make them good neighbors, good fathers and mothers, husbands and wives [and] defenders of their liberty and their country."

The Revolution spurred New England states to emancipate their slaves. The legal process began when Quork Walker sued his

Massachusetts owner for liberty. The chief justice ruled that slavery was inconsistent with the state's Declaration of Rights. By 1804 New Jersey became the last northern state to release its slaves. Emancipation was urged on by northern white laborers who resented having to compete with unpaid slave labor.

The American Revolution also stirred white antislavery voices in the South. George Mason, the slave owner who wrote Virginia's Bill of Rights, saw bondage as a threat to free government. "Every master of slaves is born a petty tyrant," he said. Mason saw bondage as capable of injuring entire communities:

> Slavery discourages arts and manufactures. The poor despise labor when performed by slaves. They prevent the immigration of whites, who really enrich and strengthen a country.

When Lafayette toured America from 1824 to 1825, Blacks welcomed him as a voice for their freedom.

But as the value of cotton and slaves rose, antislavery Southerners had to hold their tongues or be driven out of their homes. Washington, Jefferson, and other slaveholders hoped

Slave auctions, often separating mothers from their children, began to stir the conscience of the nation.

bondage would end but took no public action. Patrick Henry had announced his creed when he said, "Give me liberty or give me death!" As a slavemaster he felt trapped in a dilemma:

> Would anyone believe that I am Master of slaves of
> my own purchase. I am drawn along by the general
> inconvenience of living without them; I will not,
> I cannot justify it.

Anthony Benezet, Antislavery Huguenot

Born to Huguenot parents in France in 1713, Anthony Benezet moved to England at 16 and soon joined the Quakers. At the age of 18 Benezet immigrated to Philadelphia and began to devote his time to fighting slavery. He also denounced the mistreatment of Indians and urged education for women.

Benezet argued that the popular notion that people of color were mentally inferior was "a vulgar prejudice, founded on . . . pride or ignorance." This did not make him many friends in the white community.

He began schools to prove that nonwhites have "as great a variety of talents as amongst a like number of whites."

Benezet lectured and wrote three books about the achievements of Native Americans and African Americans. Franklin and Jefferson said his reasoned arguments had a great impact on their thinking. In 1783, the year before he died, Benezet asked signers of the Declaration of Independence how slaveholders could write their names below the words "all men are created equal." ■

CHAPTER 19

AMERICAN CULTURAL FIGURES

A distinctly American culture began to emerge during the colonial and revolutionary era. It began with poetry and travel accounts, often written by women and ethnic minorities. Anne Bradstreet's, *The Tenth Muse*, a book of verses, was published in 1650. In 1680 Jasper Danckaerts arrived from Holland and began to write descriptions of his visits to New England and New York. Slaves Phillis Wheatley and Jupiter Hammon wrote books of poetry. A Boston teacher, Sarah Kemble Knight, wrote a *Journal* about her unchaperoned horseback ride to New York.

William Douglass was a physician born in Scotland. In 1718 he settled in Boston and began to write innovative works on colonial medical practices. From France, Hector St. John de Crevecoeur visited the Great Lakes, Ohio valley, and in 1769 settled in New York. His popular *Letters from an American Farmer*, published in 1782, described life on the frontier. The New World, he said, had turned poor peasants into farmers and made Americans of its immigrants.

In 1783 Thomas Wengierski, a noted Polish poet, wrote a diary of his meetings with George Washington and other revolutionary heroes. In 1789 Gustavus Vasa, an African, wrote a chilling account of his voyage as a slave ship passenger coming from Nigeria to the Americas. He became a noted voice against slavery.

Philip Freneau, born in New York City to French parents, became a journalist and the first great American poet. In 1771 when he graduated from Princeton University he was pro-British. He hoped to see British flags flying from the Atlantic to the Pacific. By 1775 in his poetry Freneau had called the English bullies "who would bind us in chains." He enthusiastically promoted American patriotism and sought to discourage any dependence on England. Freneau enlisted as a private in the Continental army and was cap-

Poet Philip Freneau, born to French parents, raised his voice for "freedom's side."

tured. Held on a British prison ship, his suffering only strengthened his devotion to the principles of the Revolution.

After the war, Freneau used his sharp wit to lash out at any who opposed American democracy or the French Revolution. He scoffed at aristocrats and urged an economic democracy:

> How can we call those systems just
> Which bid the few, the proud, the first,
> Possess all earthly good;
> While millions robbed of all that's dear
> In silence shed the ceaseless tear,
> And leeches suck their blood . . . .

Thomas Jefferson and James Madison asked Freneau to serve as editor of the *National Gazette*, a pro-Republican paper, to counter Alexander Hamilton's pro-Federalist *The United States Gazette*. Subsequently, Freneau launched a newspaper battle against the Federalists and President Washington.

Some believed Freneau to be overly sarcastic, but others saw him as the country's greatest editor. Jefferson said he "has saved our Constitution which was fast galloping into monarchy." In one of his last poems Freneau announced he was

> . . . still on Freedom's side;
> Still in the cause of man severely true.

In 1796 John Daly Burke had to flee political persecution in Ireland. In Boston he warmly embraced his new country and its commitment to freedom. Burke wrote:

> From the moment a stranger puts his feet on the soil
> of America, his fetters are rent in pieces and the scale
> of servitude which he had contracted under European
> tyrannies fall off; he becomes a free man, and . . .
> virtually, a citizen.

Burke authored an early and patriotic play, *Bunker Hill*. In Boston he edited the city's first daily paper, and in New York he started a Jeffersonian paper.

Benjamin Banneker

Benjamin Banneker was born in colonial Maryland to an indentured Irish servant and a free African American. He educated himself and became fascinated by science. As a teenager he constructed the first clock made entirely of American parts.

For ten years, in the 1790s, Banneker published popular almanacs that provided important knowledge about the sun, moon, stars, and seasons. His almanacs also included political essays. He used these to begin a correspondence with Jefferson in which he tried to have him publicly denounce slavery.

Banneker served on the commission that planned the new federal city of Washington, D.C. Along with Pierre L'Enfant, the French citizen who had overall direction of the project, he helped select locations for the leading federal buildings, such as the Capitol and the White House. ■

David Rittenhouse

No family knew better than the Rittenhouses that the United States was a land of liberty and opportunity. In the 17th century David Rittenhouse's German-born great-grandfather became the country's first papermaker and then its first Mennonite bishop. David Rittenhouse, born in 1732 in Pennsylvania followed in these footsteps.

David's mother became a Quaker at a time when this often meant persecution. At eleven, David was a self-educated but sickly lad. He liked to read the scientific works of Isaac Newton and Benjamin Franklin. He built a workshop where he spent time puttering with his inventions.

David became a clock maker. He then developed his own telescope, surveying instruments, and the first American compass. Rittenhouse surveyed the famous Mason-Dixon Line. In 1769, using his own telescope, Rittenhouse estimated the sun to be 92,940,000 miles from Earth. Today scientists say it is 92,900,000 miles.

Rittenhouse served in Pennsylvania's Constitutional Convention and for four years directed the United States Mint. He succeeded Benjamin Franklin as president of the American Philosophical Society. He had traveled far in the land of the free. ■

John Peter Zenger

Born in Germany in 1697, at age 13 John Peter Zenger sailed to New York City. He was trained as a printer by William Bradford, publisher of the *New York Gazette* and a supporter of Governor William Cosby.

The governor was not popular. He disfranchised the Quakers, awarded himself land grants, and used public funds for his own purposes. Opposition to his brazen illegalities was led by the city's merchants and craftsmen organized in the Popular party.

In 1733 the party helped Zenger launch the *New York Weekly Journal* to expose the governor's corruption. The printer could hardly keep up with the demand for his paper. In a year the

Peter Zenger's papers are burned.

Popular party, aided by Zenger's paper, swept the city elections. An infuriated Governor Cosby asked the Assembly to indict Zenger, but it refused. He asked the Grand Jury to indict, but it also refused. Finally, Cosby had his Provincial Council order Zenger's arrest for "seditious libels."

For a week Zenger was locked in solitary confinement, and not allowed to talk to anyone or receive visitors. His bail was set at ten times the value of his possessions. Finally, he was permitted to speak with his wife through his cell door. During his months in prison, she courageously continued to publish the *New York Weekly Journal.*

Zenger twice found lawyers and twice Cosby's chief justice disbarred them. Finally, Andrew Hamilton, 79, a distinguished Philadelphia attorney, volunteered to take Zenger's case. Hamilton argued that Zenger's charges were not libel since they were the truth. At stake, Hamilton told the jury, was the "cause of liberty . . . of exposing and opposing arbitrary power." The prosecution stated that no one had a right to publish attacks on government officials even if they were completely true. Found not guilty, Zenger left a crowded, cheering courtroom.

In 1736 Zenger printed the trial record. It sold widely in the colonies and in Europe. In 1770 as American colonists began to demand their lawful, natural rights, it was reprinted again. ■

CHAPTER 20

"THE REIGN OF THE WITCHES"

Less than 100 days after George Washington was inaugurated as the first U.S. president in April 1789, France erupted in revolution. Americans at first rejoiced at the overthrow of France's ancient monarchy. In 1793 Jefferson said, "All the old spirit of 1776 is rekindling."

The mood soon changed, however. Political parties were developing in the United States, and the Federalist Party favored a more aristocratic form of government. The Federalists saw the Jacobins, or French revolutionaries, as enemies. They feared their ideas of equality for all. As the revolution in France turned more violent and more anti-aristocratic, the Federalists became more alarmed. They began to call the members of the Democratic-Republican Party, which supported Thomas Jefferson and who favored the French, "Jacobins" and "dangerous aliens."

Washington served two terms as president of the United States, but in 1796 he decided not to run for the presidency again. John Adams ran for the presidency as a Federalist, and Thomas Jefferson ran as a Democratic-Republican.

Jefferson's strongest supporters were refugees from Ireland, France, and other European nations. These foreigners now came under Federalist suspicion for their pro-democratic ideas. The first Jefferson club to be formed was the German Republican Society of Philadelphia. The group known as United Irishmen, who enthusiastically promoted French ideals, also supported Jefferson. The election campaign was hard fought and nasty, and, in the end, Jefferson lost to Adams, but became the vice president.

In 1798 when both British and French ships harassed U.S. commerce at sea, President Adams chose to bring the country into what he called a "half war" with France. Federalists then used the war scare to attack their political foes. They charged that the United

Irishmen had "organized treason" and denounced the Jeffersonians as "the French party." Jefferson's Republicans, said President Adams, were loyal to "a foreign nation" and "deserve all our contempt." A Federalist paper warned that, "Traitors must be silenced."

In one month in 1798 the Federalists swept four Alien and Sedition acts through a Congress they controlled. One gave the President authority to arrest and deport without evidence or trial any alien he suspected of "treasonable or secret inclinations."

The Sedition Act provided five years in prison and a fine of $1,000 for anyone who insulted the president, his administration, Congress, the courts, or laws. The Bill of Rights suddenly seemed nullified by the broad powers of the new laws.

New York Congressman Edward Livingston, whose ancestors came from Scotland, led a counterattack. He claimed the new laws violated the Constitution and made the president an arbitrary ruler. His point was that the Federalists sought "to excite fervor against foreign aggression only to establish a tyranny at home." Livingston saw Americans facing peril from their government:

Edus Livingston

Edward Livingston bravely denounced the first political witch-hunt.

A careless word, perhaps misrepresented, or never spoken, may be sufficient evidence; a look may destroy, an idle gesture may insure punishment.

The Federalists turned up the political fire. They claimed that "incendiary immigrants" were contaminating "the purity and simplicity of the American character." One paper urged treating Jeffersonians "as we should a TURK, A JEW, A JACOBIN, OR A DOG." The foreign born were the first to face public suspicion and hostility. Citizens were told not to hire French tutors or sing French songs. While most of the 30,000 French who lived in the United States opposed the revolution's violence, hundreds now boarded ships for France, French islands in the West Indies, or any other safe haven.

Fear escalated, and charges became more vague. Secretary of State Pickering, the chief legal officer of the United States, announced his plan to prosecute "the discontented characters which infest our country." He investigated "secret projects" of the United Irishmen and began to scrutinize Jeffersonian papers. The Sedition

Act was used to strike at Republican leaders and their journals. Indictments were issued against fifteen anti-Federalist editors. To Jefferson this period became "the reign of the witches."

Vermont congressman Matthew Lyon, born in Ireland, said he would be the first victim, and he was. An American success story, he founded Fairhaven, Vermont, fought in the Revolution, gained wealth, and married the Vermont governor's daughter. Lyon's crime was that he edited a strongly Jeffersonian paper. "Ragged Mat, the democrat," as his foes called him, was convicted of insulting President Adams. His sentence was four months imprisonment and a fine of $1,000. In a dark, damp cell Lyon continued to write editorials criticizing the administration. From prison Lyon also won overwhelming reelection to Congress.

Violence by citizens accompanied the government persecution. Irish American William Duane was one of several Jeffersonian editors to have their offices assaulted by mobs.

The first American political witch-hunt lasted two years. Federalist charges against foreigners and violations of the Bill of Rights backfired. In its haste to make scapegoats of Jefferson's supporters, the Federalist Party destroyed itself.

Thomas Jefferson was elected to the presidency in 1800, the Federalist Party soon disappeared forever. But the country had learned some frightening lessons. The Bill of Rights was only as strong as its defenders. Some politicians in high office were capable of concocting accusations of disloyalty and subversion to defeat their political foes. During a time of war or domestic tension, the foreign-born could easily become targets of bigots.

Thomas Jefferson willingly accepted support from Irish Americans, French Americans, and others, who were denounced as "dangerous aliens" by the Federalists.

Albert Gallatin, Swiss Immigrant

Years before the war fever began, one Federalist target had been Albert Gallatin, a naturalized citizen. Because he strongly represented Jeffersonian radicals in Congress, Federalists proposed a constitutional amendment to ban naturalized citizens from Congress or the presidency. It failed to pass, but it encouraged feelings that the foreign-born were untrustworthy.

Born in Geneva, Switzerland, in 1761, Albert Gallatin was an orphan at 9. But his relatives made sure he had a good education. At 19 he settled in Pennsylvania.

Gallatin began his political career when he was elected to the state's Constitutional Convention and then to the legislature. In 1793 he was elected to the U.S. Senate. From that forum he publicly asked Federalist Party leader and Secretary of the Treasury Alexander Hamilton to show how government finances had been handled. From then on the Federalists counted Gallatin among their leading foes and wanted to get rid of him.

Less than a year later the Federalist majority warned of dangerous foreigners. They charged that though he had lived in the U.S. for thirteen years, he was not properly naturalized as a citizen. As a result of their persecution, Gallatin lost his Senate seat. But in 1795 Gallatin returned when he won election as a U.S. representative from Pennsylvania. He became a leading anti-Federalist voice.

Washington and Hamilton led the U.S. Army into Pennsylvania to crush a rebellion by farmers who made their own liquor and refused to pay federal taxes. Gallatin warned the local "Whiskey Rebellion" farmers of this and urged them to destroy their stills and avoid an armed conflict. Hamilton was furious. The Federalists wanted to instill fear of the new government among the poor. Hamilton's strategy was to overawe the farmers with military power, but Gallatin had managed to frustrate his master plan.

In 1800 Jefferson was elected president. When Gallatin was made secretary of the treasury, he reduced the national debt. Then he used federal funds to serve Jeffersonian rather than Federalist goals. Gallatin continued in President Madison's cabinet where he brought order to federal finances.

During the War of 1812, Gallatin traveled to Russia on a peace mission for the president. Then he later helped draw up the Treaty of Ghent that ended the war.

One of the brightest American statesmen of his day, Gallatin served his nation for half a century. He also became an expert on and defender of Native Americans. In 1842 he founded the American Ethnological Society to promote studies of Native American life. ■

CHAPTER 21

LOUISIANA AND THE FUR TRADE

In 1803 President Jefferson purchased the Louisiana Territory from France for $15,000,000 or about four cents an acre. The sale doubled the size of the country and would add thirteen new states. But it ignored the fact that, although Napoleon may have sold it, it was Native Americans who lived there and claimed it.

Originally, Jefferson wanted to buy only New Orleans, but Napoleon suddenly offered to sell the entire Louisiana Territory. In Haiti his forces had suffered stunning military defeats at the hands of slaves and had to abandon their plans for a North American empire.

To explore the new territory, President Jefferson dispatched Meriwether Lewis and William Clark. Among the 42 men they assembled was York, Clark's slave. Both age 23, Clark and York had grown up together. At a time when most men were under five foot five, York was over six feet in height and 200 pounds in weight. The expedition's interpreter was a French Canadian, Toussaint Charbonneau. He was accompanied by his 16-year-old Shoshoni wife, Sacajawea, who carried her new baby on her back.

Sacajewea and the 42 men began to wend their way through the forests, streams, and mountains of the northwest. As translator Sacajewea was assisted by York who demonstrated formidable skills as an interpreter. He also became the party's ambassador of good will to Indian nations that had never seen so large and agile a black man.

York and Sacajewea were able to build good relations with Native Americans. By the end of 1805 the two won the right to vote on crucial issues with the rest of the explorers.

After two and a half years the expedition returned from Oregon's Pacific coast to St. Louis with tales of mountains teeming with valuable beaver and of Indians willing to trade. The Missouri River, the expedition found, made these hunting grounds easily accessible.

The next major expedition into the Louisiana Territory was led in 1807 by Manuel Lisa, a Spaniard. It included the awesome Edward Rose, a thick-set African Cherokee with a slashed nose, scarred forehead, and fierce look. To Indians he was "Cutnose." Washington Irving described him as "powerful in frame and fearless in spirit." Rose was also fluent in twelve native languages.

The Lisa expedition returned with the news that large fur companies rather than individual traders would produce the greatest profits. The trade in pelts and skins became big business and Lisa and Rose became its experts at wilderness operations.

Rose went on to serve as a guide, hunter, and interpreter for the Missouri Fur Company, the Rocky Mountain Fur Company, and the American Fur Company. He was joined by French Canadians, African Americans, Highland Scots and a host of other European

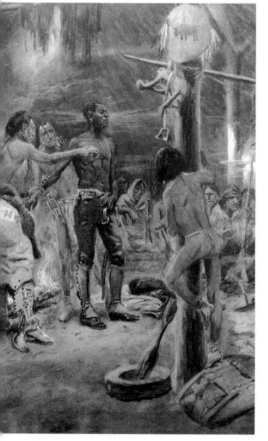

adventurers. The trade still depended on Native Americans though to supply it with furs.

In 1808 John Jacob Astor, a German-born financier, entered the trade. Over the next four decades Astor's American Fur Company, through its control of trade in the Great Lakes region, became one of the nation's leading commercial concerns.

Four decades after Lewis and Clark, American trappers of every race and nation had helped tame the Louisiana Territory. But these rough, uncouth, unshaven men did something else of lasting significance. They discovered more rivers and mountain passes than all the U.S. government expeditions sent for that purpose. The trappers accomplished this feat without trying and largely by accident. They were seeking furs in the shortest time and speeding them back to their customers in the East.

The Mandan Indians meet York as seen in this mural by Charles Russell.

CHAPTER 22

THE WAR OF 1812

The War of 1812 with England was preceded by a series of United States conflicts with Native Americans. In 1808 Chief Tecumseh and his brother, Tenskwatawa the Prophet, tried to unite Native American nations from the Great Lakes to Florida. They urged rejection of European liquor, guns, and trade. Indian leaders must also refuse to sell land to whites. "Any sale not made by all is not valid," Tecumseh declared.

To build an alliance, the chief visited Indian nations in the United States and Canada. He met with the five Native American nations of the South—the Chickasaws, Choctaws, Creeks, Cherokees, and Seminoles. He rode west to the Delawares, Shawnees, and Osages, then northward to the Sauk and Fox and the Black Hawks.

When Tecumseh returned home in 1812 his Pan-Indian union had only begun. But his own people were allied with England and at war with the United States of America. He reluctantly coordinated attacks with British commanders. His troops quickly captured Detroit.

In "The Battle of the Thames" a white artist depicts the European war with Native Americans.

By 1813, Tecumseh led more than 3,000 soldiers from 32 Native American nations. The British placed Colonel Henry Proctor over these forces. Proctor, a frightened man, at one point ordered his Indian troops to massacre prisoners. An infuriated Tecumseh halted the slaughter and told Proctor, "I conquer to save, and you to murder." But within a year Tecumseh died in battle and with him his plan to unify Native American nations of many regions.

White Americans faced trouble on another front as slave rebels became more active. In January 1811, the largest insurrection in the United States struck Louisiana's St. John the Baptiste Parish, 36 miles from New Orleans. From the Andry estate 500 armed Blacks, including Charles Deslondes, a free Black from Haiti, marched on the city.

Officers of the rebellion carried flags and orderly companies marched to drum beats. The rebels destroyed five plantations picking up recruits along the way. General Wade Hampton raced 600 militiamen into the field. A panicky governor summoned additional federal troops. This combined force converged on and defeated the rebels, executing 68 it considered leaders. However, some insurrectionists were able to flee. Fear of uprisings grew in the Louisiana Territory as escaped slaves reach safety among the British and Native Americans. A U.S. officer reported, "Our Negroes are flocking to the enemy from all quarters." As troops they had, he complained, "the most minute knowledge of every bypath [and they] return upon us as guides."

The United States counted on its minorities to help defeat the British in the War of 1812. After the enemy burned Washington, D.C., Philadelphians thought they might be next. James Forten, Bishop Richard Allen, and Reverend Absolom Jones recruited 2,500 other free African American residents to fortify the city.

U.S. officers and soldiers in the war included thousands of recent immigrants from Ireland, Germany, Poland, Canada, Sweden, Denmark, Italy, and other European nations. One-sixth of the U.S. Navy were African Americans, and many others were descendants of European immigrants.

Benjamin Nones, a hero of the Revolutionary War, was among eight Jewish American officers. His son Joseph served under Stephen Decatur on the *Guerriere* and later at the Ghent peace conference that ended the war. At Williamsburg, Virginia, Captain Mordecai Myers led a successful charge against British positions. In the decisive battle at Plattsburg, New York, an army of white and Black Americans drove back 14,000 British troops. However, the most significant American victory took place at New Orleans. Andrew Jackson recruited a unique army. First, he appealed to the slave population, and they agreed to build his defenses. The French

Jewish pirate Jean LaFitte agreed to round up his motley crew, some from the city's jails. Choctaw Indians in full war paint formed a company. White business and professional men, some with thick European accents, arrived for battle with their own muskets.

When Jackson promised the city's free people of color equal pay and treatment, 500 volunteered. One black force included merchants, craftsmen, and laborers. Another black battalion was made up of recent refugees from Haiti's revolution. Jackson boasted to Emperor Napoleon of his decisive victory, "My riflemen killed and wounded 2,117 in less than an hour . . . . I lost 6 killed and 7 wounded." As Jackson reported, British General Pakenham was slain by "a free man of color, who was a famous rifle-shot."

For the United States the War of 1812 proved to be an historical turning point. The British Empire failed to regain its colonies. The last invasion of the United States of America had been decisively thrown back. European nations now had to respect the military might and government of the new republic. Moreover, in the West the federal government inflicted a series of defeats on Native Americans who had sided with the British. Indian power had been broken, and the frontier beckoned to new settlers.

To defend New Orleans, men of three races united.

FURTHER READING

Adamic, Louis. *A Nation of Nations*. New York: Harper, 1944.

Bernado, Stephanie. *The Ethnic Almanac*. New York: Dolphin, 1981.

The Council on Interracial Books for Children, ed. *Chronicles of American Indian Protest*. Greenwich, CT: Fawcett Publications, 1971.

Debo, Angie. *A History of the Indians of the United States*, rev. ed. Norman, OK: University of Oklahoma Press, 1984.

The Ethnic Chronology Series. Dobbs Ferry, NY: Oceana Publications, 1972–1990.

Franklin, John Hope. *From Slavery to Freedom*, rev. ed. New York: Alfred A. Knopf, 1988.

Handlin, Oscar. *The Uprooted*. New York: Grosset & Dunlap, 1951.

The *In America* Series. Minneapolis, MN: Lerner Publications, 1971–1990.

Katz, William Loren. *Black Indians: A Hidden Heritage*. New York: Atheneum Publishers, 1990.

Millstein, Beth and Bodin, Jeanne, eds. *We, the American Women; A Documentary History*, New York: Ozer Publishing, 1977.

Moquin, Wayne, ed. *A Documentary History of the Mexican Americans*. New York: Bantam, 1972.

Myers, Gustavus. *History of Bigotry in the United States*. New York: Capricorn Books, 1960.

Seller, Maxine S. *To Seek America: A History of Ethnic Life in the United States*. New York: Ozer Publishing, 1977.

Shannon, William V. *The American Irish*. New York: Macmillan, 1964.

Thernstrom, Stephan, ed. *Harvard Encyclopedia of American Ethnic Groups*. Cambridge, MA: Harvard University Press, 1980.

INDEX

9-21-95